THE THIRD HEAVEN

and the unutterable things that can now be told

JIM STRAHAN

WESTBOW
PRESS®
A DIVISION OF THOMAS NELSON
& ZONDERVAN

WestBow Press books may be ordered through booksellers or by contacting:

WestBow Press
A Division of Thomas Nelson & Zondervan
1663 Liberty Drive
Bloomington, IN 47403
www.westbowpress.com
844-714-3454

Edited by Taylor Burnfield

Interior Image Credit: Depositphotos Inc.

ISBN: 979-8-3850-2073-7 (sc)
ISBN: 979-8-3850-2074-4 (e)

Library of Congress Control Number: 2024904584

Print information available on the last page.

WestBow Press rev. date: 03/06/2024

CONTENTS

INTRODUCTION

As I embarked on the task of documenting God's grace in my life, I also made a request to our Heavenly Father to share something new with fellow believers. My narrative is but one of the countless stories throughout history bearing witness to God's presence and the depth of His love for all. However, beyond merely joining their ranks, I harbored an aspiration to contribute something new from His Word, aiming to honor Him even more and to offer encouragement to others.

Following that last prayer request, and just before disseminating the text of my story to others, another series of remarkable events unfolded, almost immediately. Consequently, at the eleventh hour I incorporated additional insights about Paul's experience when he was caught up to the third heaven. Seven years later, and quite unexpectedly, that topic flourished into a significant theme I have discovered throughout the Bible, spanning from Genesis to Revelation. I am confident that God answered my prayer, and He surpassed my expectations. Moreover, I believe He intends for me to share this information with you.

I pray this manuscript will serve as an adequate introduction to the topic. I believe that once exposed to what has been hidden in plain sight in His Word, many will be able to expand upon it. Our Father is an incredibly brilliant writer and teacher. Upon gaining enlightenment from Him, you may find yourself asking the same question I repeatedly posed to myself: *How could I have missed this for so long?*

However, this topic may present some challenges, as it diverges from some of the more widely accepted eschatology—the doctrines or beliefs concerning the end of the present age, human history, or the world itself. Nevertheless, fret not, because this groundbreaking material may offer an even more comforting perspective than what many of us Christians have previously been taught about the final outcome. God, in Ephesians 2:7, foretold that in the ages to come, the richness of His grace in His kindness would surpass our expectations. True to His prophetic Word, what He has presented here has undoubtedly exceeded my own, and I am confident it will do the same for many others.

I will begin by establishing a foundation through a discussion of three resurrections. Subsequently, I will draw connections to the three heavens. I am confident that you will find this pattern of threes to be as fascinating as it is ubiquitous throughout His Word. I will address only twenty-five of the more evident instances in the scriptures that point to the three groups to be resurrected, and I trust others will uncover many more. As we are about to see, there are substantial reasons why the number three appears 467 times in the Bible, nearly as frequently as the number seven.

Given my human nature, certain parts of this narrative may not be flawless, but I do not believe my brothers and sisters in Christ will hold my shortcomings against me. Instead, I pray that the richness of God's kindness will somehow shine through my humble attempt at expressing the enormity of His goodness and love for us. I trust that the outcome will enhance our affections for Him and deepen our trust in His plans.

I believe our heavenly Father is keen on establishing a deeply personal relationship with each of us. While fellow believers should consistently guide others toward Him, I do not believe He desires a relationship solely based on what someone else has said about Him. Instead, I think He seeks direct communication with each of us.

Much like any caring parent, I am convinced that He delights in hearing the voices of His children, and He desires for us to know and experience His voice firsthand. Therefore, what I say, or others may say about this topic, is not as important as what He communicates to you about it. Just as a mentor of mine, Dr. J.V. Foster, instructed me in my youth, when reading a book concerning God's Word, look for the golden nuggets our Father has left there for you. As you peruse this manuscript, I pray you will hear His voice and enjoy His companionship.

At the conclusion of each chapter, He might pose to each of us the same question He asked His disciples: *Who do you say I am?* I pray that the contents of this book will contribute to our responses. I hope it will expand our list of reasons why we can, and should, appreciate His love—the driving force behind His boundless power, wisdom, and knowledge.

Our Hope and
Assurance in Christ

SOMEONE ONCE EXPRESSED that grief is the price of love when we lose someone close and dear to us. Although it is an experience nearly all of us will encounter at some point in our lives, as Christians, we are not left without hope. Matthew 5:4 assures us that those who mourn will be comforted, and a significant part of that assurance comes from knowing that we will be reunited with our loved ones.

Similarly, recording artist Big Daddy Weave sang about this very topic in his song "Heaven Changes Everything." I love the words in the second verse, where he sang about how the goodbyes to our loved ones would not be the end. Indeed, "Heaven Changes Everything."

In my quest to understand Christian beliefs regarding our future resurrections to a new life in heaven, I delved into various well-regarded Bible commentaries and examined statements of faith from some of the largest Christian denominations. The statements of faith I studied originated from Catholic, Lutheran, Methodist, Baptist, Presbyterian, Anglican, Episcopal, and Assembly of God organizations. While there are certainly other denominations to explore, these provided me with a good overview of the Christian perspective on the subject.

As I examined them, it became abundantly clear that the prevailing belief among Christians is that our journey to paradise reaches its culmination in victory through one or two major resurrection events. Clearly, not all of them shared a consensus on the timing, nor the individuals involved in each resurrection. Nevertheless, I was pleasantly surprised by the openness and willingness to accommodate differing opinions.

As an example, I came across instances where many Catholics believe that resurrection takes place at the time of death. However, there are other Catholics, following the understanding of the late Pope Benedict XVI, who believe that resurrection occurs at the conclusion of history during the general judgment.

On a Presbyterian site, I learned that according to their perspective, when one dies, the soul goes to either heaven or hell, and during the final judgment, bodies are reunited with their souls. This notion appears to be widely embraced among Christians. However, Luther and Tyndale would strongly disagree. They placed their belief in Ezekiel 18:20, which asserts that souls that sin shall die, echoing God's message to Adam and Eve in the garden. Consequently, they preached that the deceased are presently in a state of "sleep" in the grave, anticipating the "redemption of our bodies," as mentioned in Romans 8:23. Additionally, they subscribed to the idea that our physical resurrection from the dead will mirror the pattern of our Lord's resurrection.

While these opinions were intriguing, my intention here is not to encompass all the diverse beliefs surrounding this captivating topic, nor to advocate for any specific viewpoint. At this juncture, I solely aim to underscore one particularly interesting aspect—how the majority of the 30-plus sources I perused firmly adhere to a belief in either one or two future resurrection events that will finalize our eternal destinies. In the following paragraphs, I will present an overview of the scriptures used to substantiate these beliefs, along with the various interpretations of the individuals involved in each resurrection event.

The prevailing belief is that there will be two resurrections, with some suggesting that the first is designated for the saved (believers), and the second for the unsaved (non-believers). However, the more widely accepted perspective, among those advocating for two resurrections, involves the participation of the saved in both. This viewpoint primarily stems from an interpretation of Revelation 20:4-6 and John 5:28-29, where they identify two distinct harvests of souls. The first one in Revelation declares:

"And I saw the souls of those who had been beheaded because of the testimony for Jesus and because of the word of God. They had not worshipped the beast or his image and had not received his mark on their foreheads or their hands. They came to life and reigned with Christ a thousand years. (The rest of the dead did not come to life until the thousand years were ended.) This is the first resurrection. Blessed and holy are those who have a part in the first resurrection. The second death has no power over them, but they will be priests of God and of Christ and will reign with him for a thousand years" (NIV).

In these scriptures, we read about "souls" being made alive in the "first resurrection." Afterward, they reign with Christ for "a thousand years," and the remainder of the dead do not come to life until the end of that time period. That last part, concerning the rest of the dead, is understood by many to be the second resurrection. Furthermore, John 5:28-29 is used to provide a few more details concerning the second one:

"Do not marvel at this; for the hour is coming when all who are in the tombs will hear his voice and come forth; those who have done good, to the resurrection of life and those who have done evil, to the resurrection of judgment" (RSV).

Obviously, this cannot pertain to the first resurrection, because that one was limited. Revelation 20:12-15 is also used to give us more insight into the second one:

"And I saw the dead, the great and small, standing before the throne, and the books were opened. Also, another book was opened, which is the book of life. And the dead were judged by what was written in the books, by what they had done. . . Then Death and Hades were thrown into the lake of fire. This is the second death, the lake of fire; and if anyone's name was not found written in the book of life, he was thrown into the lake of fire" (RSV).

In this passage, we find the "hour" comes when all who are in the tombs are raised either to life, or to judgment, with the latter experiencing the lake of fire, the second death. It appears the saved, who were not resurrected in the first one, are raised in the second, along with all the unsaved.

I also read another opinion from a well-respected author and scholar who leans toward an understanding that both these resurrections refer to the same event. However, the word "first" implies that at least one more follows. Also, "the rest of the dead," do not come to life with the first group "until" the end of a long period of time, "a thousand years."

For these reasons, it is very difficult for me to follow the logic in a belief in only one resurrection. However, we can all come together in thanksgiving to our Father that at the end of either scenario, believers will be resurrected to life, whether it is one or two. Thank you, Lord!

Whether we believe in one or two, Paul provides some additional information with the following from 1 Thessalonians 4:16-18:

> "For the Lord Himself shall descend from heaven. . . and the dead in Christ shall rise first. Then, we which are alive and remain, shall be caught up together with them in the clouds to meet the Lord in the air: and so shall we ever be with the Lord" (KJV).

Those words are certainly in line with John's understanding. The dead in Christ, who participate in one or two resurrections, rise before those in Christ who are alive at His coming. Also, please note that unless we are alive at His coming, being "made alive" in these passages requires a former state of physical death – like those beheaded along with all others who were in a physical tomb.

Furthermore, Paul tells us in Thessalonians 4:13-14 not to grieve over brethren who have "fallen asleep", like the rest who do not hope. And the author of Hebrews reminds us in the first verse of chapter 11 that faith is confidence in what we hope for and assurance in what we do not yet see.

A person only harbors hope for something they currently lack. Clearly, once the expected outcome materializes, there is no longer a need for hope.

Therefore, if we presently hold hope for a resurrection, it implies that it is a future event. In other words, when Paul wrote those words of hope, he had not yet experienced a physical resurrection. As a mortal, he had not acquired immortality in the same manner as Jesus had when He was resurrected. Nevertheless, Paul had been "made alive" in another sense, and I will discuss this crucial topic in the next chapter.

So, what have I gleaned about our resurrections from all my readings? Drawing from the explicit words in John, Thessalonians, and Revelation, one can readily trace the rationale for at least two distinct resurrections. The first is limited, while the second encompasses the rest. Just as in the case of Jesus, each resurrection involves transitioning from a physical state of death, except for those who are alive at His coming.

Romans 6:5, referring to those who have been baptized into Christ Jesus, "shall certainly be united with him in a resurrection like his" (Nestle-Aland). Similar to His resurrection, ours will entail being adorned with immortality through a new, imperishable body. It's important to note: Jesus received a new body at His resurrection, not thousands of years later.

As I looked over each article and opinion regarding who was or was not involved in each resurrection, I genuinely valued the insights each teacher brought to the table. But what would happen if there were another resurrection occurring after the two described above? Pardon the pun, but this would pose a "grave" problem, because regardless of whether the writer believed in one or two resurrections, and whether they believed the saved are involved in one or both, they were all unwavering in their assertion that afterwards, the eternal destiny for every person would be set in stone with no possibility of change from that point forward.

According to these expositors, all "believers" are destined for an eternal presence in heaven, while all "non-believers" will face either extermination, or perpetual conscious torment, based on their version of the first or second resurrection. If this is accurate, what would be the rationale for a third resurrection happening much later? Clearly, based on their interpretation, there would be no perceived necessity for one, therefore, there could not be another.

As one of these commentators, referring to Matthew 10:28, Luke 12:4-5, Luke 16:23, Revelation 14:9-11, and Revelation 20:14, articulated in a position paper adopted by the Assemblies of God in August 17, 1976: "None of these passages indicates any promise of rehabilitation or restoration once the final judgment is pronounced. No sanctifying agent is revealed in connection with the lake of fire or Gehenna. The fire is parallel to the worm of Mark 9:44,46,48 (KJV)." This is why, at least for them, there can be no resurrection after the judgment found in the second resurrection – Assemblies of God (USA) Official Web Site | Eternal Punishment.

However, in the remainder of this book, my intention is to demonstrate how the Bible does indeed teach a third physical resurrection from the dead. And once this additional resurrection is acknowledged, there will be a need to re-examine some of our presuppositions concerning the outcome of God's plans. Sufficient confirmation will be uncovered from the scriptures to make these points reasonable and evident, literally spanning from Genesis to Revelation.

Realizing the enormity of the subject, and the years of study and prayer it took for me to see it plainly in His Word, I see the need for a slow and cautious approach in this book. Ultimately, Jesus is our teacher, and we need to be respectful of what He has planned for every student during their individual classroom experiences.

Also, I have learned from a lifetime of experiences that He provided, some resistance to change occurs in almost all aspects of human endeavors, including in business, politics, science, and yes, religion too. As a retired Industrial Engineer, I recall one of our mottos: "Sell, don't tell." When it became necessary to implement changes in any operation to enhance safety and productivity, sometimes it required a few lengthy meetings with those on the ground who were actually performing the work. Explanations had to be given and discussed in detail before the changes could be made. This process played a vital role in the overall success of any operational improvements. During those discussions, receiving input from all members of the team often led to even more ideas to enhance the workplace. Buy-in from everyone was what we sought, and hopefully, that is my intention here as well.

In the process of sharing what I believe God has given me, if I offend anyone with my choice of words, please forgive me. My selection of them is not always perfect, and they may be at times, insufficient. For instance, in chapters 5 and 6, I will do a closer examination of "the fire" and "the worm" mentioned in the above quote from the Assemblies of God. I do not intend to be disrespectful to those who were genuinely conveying their understanding of it, but I believe many will be surprised to discover that the Old Testament informs us that Jesus was the worm, and the fervor of God's love is the fire that never gives up, will not fail, and is consequently described in some verses as unquenchable.

My explanation of those verses may come across too strongly, but please understand that I did not know these things for most of my life either, and I got very excited and emotionally charged when another of God's teachers pointed out these facts to me. This is the awesome part of being in His classroom, because He is the best teacher ever!

In the subsequent chapters of this book, I will also need to address some of the inevitable questions that may arise, and undoubtedly, there will be many. For instance, one may wonder: How does the concept of "future resurrections" align with the context of Colossians 2:12-13 and Ephesians 2:5-7, where individuals have already been made alive? We will explore these verses in the upcoming chapter to illustrate how they speak to a quality of life that we can presently experience in our current circumstances.

Before we proceed, consider this final thought: You are probably much like me. I do not particularly enjoy facing any kind of correction, unless it is in my favor. I mean, it is tough on my old ego. I did not appreciate it as a child when my parents had to correct me, and I did not like it from teachers in school, or from coaches on the athletic field. And if the truth be told, I still do not enjoy it when my weaknesses are on full display.

In a way, I remind myself of one of the main characters in Dr. Suess' "Green Eggs and Ham." It is one of my grandson's favorite books, and I have read it so many times that I think I have memorized most of it. My "Green Eggs and Ham" moments come when I must "eat my own words" and stand corrected by another Sam-I-Am. Just like the character in that story, I do not like it here, there, or anywhere, including in my house, or from my spouse, or from instant replay not in my team's favor.

However, I have come to appreciate it when my heavenly Father corrects me, as I know He has my best interests at heart. If I remain humble before Him, the correction comes so gently and kindly that it creates wonderful and lasting memories. He knows how to do it, and it is a fundamental aspect of being in a relationship with someone who loves you and knows everything about you. He is aware of our weaknesses, yet, simultaneously, He will become our strength.

I needed correction from Him more than once as I studied this subject, and I am immensely grateful for it. Without it, I would be like a lost ball in tall weeds. Therefore, I encourage you to listen to His voice as you read this book. The main character in Dr. Suess' book eventually tried and liked "Green Eggs and Ham," and you may also find that you like the idea of three resurrections, complements of our God-I-Am.

Next, I will address what it means to be "made alive."

2

Dead Man Walking

PAUL WROTE TO the Colossians from prison and addressed the Ephesians while being "in chains," likely indicating a period of house arrest. Similarly, we might encounter situations where our earthly circumstances feel like a prison, marked by diseases, disappointments, and the looming fear of death. Nevertheless, Paul assures us that our victory in Christ is assured. He conveys that the effort to ensure our freedom and restoration has already been completed, and the outcome is guaranteed.

In Colossians 3:2, Paul urges us to direct our focus and thoughts towards heavenly matters, where our triumph is assured, rather than being preoccupied with the temporary circumstances on Earth. Additionally, in 1 Corinthians 15:54-56, he provides further encouragement regarding our future. He states that the transformation from perishable to imperishable and mortal to immortal will occur in due time, not prematurely. At that moment, the prophecy will be fulfilled: "54. Death is swallowed up in victory. . . 56. The sting of death is sin, and the power of sin is in the law" (RSV).

In his letter to the Romans, Paul explains how the old covenant, rooted in the law, resulted in death due to the inherent weakness of the flesh and our incapacity to adhere to it. However, we express gratitude to God for bestowing upon us a new covenant known as Grace, achieved through the sacrificial offering of His Son.

Paul further underscores that we "have died to the law through the body of Christ. . . Now, we are released from the law, no longer bound by what held us captive, enabling us to serve not under the old written code but in the new life of the Spirit" (Romans 7:4-6, RSV). This sentiment echoes Paul's reminder to the Christians in his letter to the Colossians, who exhibited a tendency to revert back to legalism under the law.

Based on various commentaries I have read, the prevailing scholarly view suggests that the inhabitants of Colossae were primarily Greek, with a notable Jewish presence. It seems this church was blending Greek philosophy with traditional Jewish law, and perhaps even incorporating elements of Oriental mysticism. In his letter, Paul cautions them against regressing to their former practices and urges them to maintain Christ as the focal point of their worship.

The Jewish segment faced particular challenges, and evidently, they had been urging recent Christian converts to adhere to their former legal system. Paul addressed these "colossal" issues in Colossians 2:13-16: "And you, who were dead in trespasses and the uncircumcision of your flesh, God made alive together with him, having forgiven us all our trespasses, having cancelled the bond which stood against us with its legal demands; this he set aside, nailing it to the Cross... Therefore, let no one pass judgment on you in questions of food and drink or with regard to a festival or a new moon or a sabbath" (RSV).

The elements mentioned in that final verse were regulated by the ordinances under the old covenant. Paul was emphasizing to these Jews that God had liberated them from that bond characterized by its legal requirements. Those once "dead in trespasses" experienced renewed life through forgiveness following the abolition of the old covenant. Clearly, this symbolic language was referring to the transformative impact of Jesus on the Cross.

It is important to note that Paul, and everyone else he was speaking to, would eventually experience physical death, as he was not alluding to a physical resurrection in this passage. In chapter 3, verse 1, Paul continues his exhortation, stating, "If you have been raised with Christ, seek the things that are above, where Christ is (in heavenly places), seated at the right hand of God" (RSV). If you had already been physically resurrected, you would not have to seek things that are above, because you would already be there, where Christ is in heavenly places.

This echoes the same message he conveyed to the Church in Ephesus in Ephesians 2:4-7: "But God, who is rich in mercy, out of the great love with which He loved us, **even when we were dead through our trespasses, made us alive with Christ** (by grace you have been saved), and raised us up with Him, and made us sit in heavenly places in Christ Jesus, that in the coming ages He might show the immeasurable riches of His grace in kindness toward us in Christ Jesus" (RSV).

Recall the Old Testament narrative involving the tablets of the law stored in a container known as the Ark. The Mercy Seat served as a covering for the contents, and whenever that covering was removed, people perished. This illustrated that death would be the result when there is no barrier between us and the law. This explains why the law remained veiled and was housed in a chest, or a coffin. (Yes, one of the Hebrew words for Ark is coffin, and I believe it was pointing to its future.)

Additionally, let us reflect on the incident where Uzzah lost his life while attempting to prevent the Ark from falling off the cart. This event served as another prelude to future events, underscoring the idea that humanity would be incapable of "upholding the law."

The old covenant operated as a two-sided agreement, with benefits granted to one party if it could fulfill its obligations under the agreement's terms. Recognizing the desire for us to access those benefits, our heavenly Father understood the necessity of replacing the old covenant with a new one. The new covenant would be one-sided. God, through the work of His Son, would do all that was necessary for His children to receive those benefits, including the gift of immortality.

The name Uzzah, means "might or strength," and the name given by David to the location where Uzzah met his demise – Perez-Uzzah, means "a breach of strength." The Ark, destined for its rightful location, was being transported on a man-made military cart pulled by oxen, symbols of earthly power and strength. However, God had earlier instructed that the Ark should be covered, and when taken to its proper place, it should be carried by the priesthood on poles over their shoulders.

In all of this, God was painting a vivid picture for us. Man's strength, even with any earthly program a man could devise in support of it, could not uphold the law. It required Jesus, acting as our high priest, to bear the burden of upholding the law on His shoulders. He accomplished this task, carrying it to its ultimate destination on a pole – the Cross – where He covered and nailed our sins and the old covenant of the law to it!

Once more, in those passages from Colossians and Ephesians, Paul was not discussing a physical resurrection, although he did anticipate one following his physical death. His focus was on how Jesus had liberated them from the curse of the law. Christ served as the Mercy Seat that covered the law, and in the absence of Him, anyone under the law faced death.

Jesus, the Lamb of God, "who takes away the sin of the world," includes both you, me, and Uzzah (John 1:29 – RSV). Gratefully, He lifted Israel from the perilous situation they were once entangled in. This heavenly elevation is the same place He figuratively "raised us up with Him," emphasizing the mental peace of mind we have after the realization of "by grace you have been saved."

The lyrics from that great song, "Dead Man Walking," speak about a freedom that the writer, Jeremy Camp, could not find until Christ rescued him. He sang that it was like being six feet underground from the weight of his sin, but then, Jesus gave him life, where he could breathe again. In other words, he felt like a "Dead Man Walking," until He was walking with Christ. That song reflects a wonderful testimony, and it confirms what Paul was alluding to.

The commencement of this new life hinges on recognizing what He accomplished on the Cross – delivering us from the curse of the law by pardoning and removing our sins. It unfolds as a relationship resembling a marriage, where two entities unite as one. The benefits derived from this union with Him are extraordinary, encompassing a life rich in meaning and purpose in the present age, along with the promise of resurrection and being adorned with immortality in the life to come.

Later in this book, we will discuss some Old Testament stories that highlight God's passionate love for His bride. It evoked memories of the intense emotions I experienced when I first met mine. During that time, it felt as though she occupied my thoughts constantly, and my primary desire was to spend time with her, convincing her that I was the one with whom she should spend the rest of her life.

Those special evenings together were truly enjoyable, filled with conversations, our favorite pizza, and beer. I cherished the moments riding my motorcycle with her on the back, holding me tightly, and singing to me as we navigated the scenic Texas Hill Country. Those were wonderful times, and I wonder if God feels a similar affection for us as we did for each other. I believe He does, even though His preference might be wine with His pizza.

Furthermore, in John 5:24-25, we find that Jesus was the inspiration behind the words in Jeremy's song. As He ministered to Israel, He said to them: "Truly, truly, I say to you, the hour is coming, and now is, when the dead will hear the voice of the Son of God, and those who hear will live" (RSV).

In the preceding verse, Jesus conveyed to His audience that those who heed His words will not face judgment but will transition from death to life. Jesus was not merely referring to a physical resurrection. During that period, Israel existed in a state of spiritual death because they struggled to adhere to the old covenant of the law. It was imperative for them to embrace His message of grace and recognize Him as their Savior. Doing so would enable them to lead an inspired life both individually and collectively as a nation – the life to which He had called them.

However, the majority rejected His message, leading to the nation's death at the hands of the Romans in 70 A.D. The remnant, those who truly "heard" His words, survived to fulfill their calling as instruments in His hands, spreading the good news of the gospel to the nations.

Clearly, our Lord's words continue to have relevance for us today. When we, born in sin and death due to our inherited nature from Adam, confess Jesus as our Lord and Savior, we experience a profound transformation – we are made alive! It is important to note that this transformation does not just imply immortality, but it points to a heightened quality of life, fostering a meaningful relationship with Him in the present moment.

Our baptism serves as a symbol of the burial of our old self with Christ, as we are immersed in a body of water and then raised out of it into a new life in Him. In essence, being "made alive" encompasses at least two significant aspects. First, it involves living a purpose-driven life in the present age. Second, it entails being adorned with immortality in the ages to come, mirroring the experience of Jesus. The promised resurrection, as articulated in the verses we referenced from John, Thessalonians, and Revelation, truly encapsulates the hope we possess in Christ.

I acknowledge that there are diverse interpretations of the scriptures previously mentioned, and I will strive to approach these differences with consideration and respect. Despite different views, there is common ground we can share. Regardless of our location, the timing of our beliefs, or our stance on whether we have already experienced resurrection, our guidance for living remains consistent – to love God with all our heart and to love our neighbors as ourselves. Throughout this, let's keep in mind His passion – His longing for a close relationship with each of us in the present. The rest can be considered as "icing on the cake."

These aforementioned passages also unite us through the practical insights shared by Pastor James Hollandsworth on what it truly means to be "made alive" and how we can better fulfill our calling in Him amid our current circumstances. In his book, "The Savior of All Men," he recounts the story of how our Father revealed a profound truth to him. James reflected on the initial years of his ministry as a period of stagnation, describing it as "going nowhere." Despite earnest efforts to be a devout Christian by adhering to a checklist of spiritual practices, he said he found no vibrancy; instead, he experienced regular defeat.

Later, James attended a conference where he heard an elderly gentleman emphasize the significance of relying on God's strength rather than our own. It was during this moment that James recognized how his pride manifested itself as "self-sufficiency." When faced with failure, he would intensify his efforts to succeed. It became clear to him that "God was merely my credo, not my source of strength."

Does this sound familiar? Consider Israel under the old covenant. And can you relate this to your own experiences? Have you ever felt like a failure, even after giving your best effort? I certainly have.

Then, the 6th chapter of Romans became alive for James. In verses 4-6, he discovered that just as we have been buried with Christ, we have also been made alive with Him. In verses 11-13, we acknowledge ourselves as dead to sin but alive to God in Christ. In short, **our righteousness and strength reside in Him.**

My friend, Pastor Peter Hiett, expressed it profoundly in a way that I will not easily forget: "We need to stop 'shoulding' on ourselves, stop worshipping 'Me-sus,' and start worshipping Jesus." Another writer articulated a similar sentiment: "A man's self-help will avail nothing. You can play reveille in Arlington National Cemetery for a whole year, but you will get no response from the dead soldiers there."

Hence, what I gleaned from Peter's and James' testimonies is that I must cease relying on my own strength to attain perfection. Instead, I should allow the One residing within me, the One who has already fulfilled the law, to assist me in overcoming sin and guiding me to the place He has designed for me – a heavenly place in Him. This realization was such a relief.

Struggling to overcome a particular sin? Allow the Lord within you to take charge. As Philippians 4:13 (KJV) affirms, "I can do all things through Christ which strengtheneth me." When we do conquer these challenges through Christ, our words will echo the genuine sentiments found in the latter part of Isaiah 45:23-24, just as God foretold: "That unto me every knee shall bow, every tongue shall swear. Surely, shall one say, 'in the Lord have I righteousness and strength'" (KJV).

Great news! We are no longer slaves to sin because Jesus has completed the work on our behalf. Our salvation is solely from Him, not stemming from our attempts to uphold the law but through His faith and strength, graciously provided.

Author Caleb Miller, in his book "The Divine Reversal," highlights the crucial distinction that faith (pistis) is a noun, not a verb. He also illustrated how the King James and Young's translations more accurately convey that our faith is "of Christ" not just "in Christ." This implies that our faith originates from Him, which is why it is referred to as a "gift." It is not something we generate on our own. Caleb supports this perspective by citing Galatians 2:16, 2:20, 3:14, 3:22, 1 Timothy 1:14, Philippians 3:8-9, and Romans 3:22 as proof texts from the KJV and YLT.

Furthermore, Ephesians 2:8-9 states this concept clearly and succinctly: "For by grace, you have been saved through faith, **and that not of yourselves;** it is the gift of God, not of works, lest anyone should boast" (KJV). Armed with this understanding, Romans 4:4-5 has become one of my favorite passages: "Now when a man works, his wages are not credited to him as a gift but as an obligation. However, to the man who does not work (at all) but trusts God, who justifies the wicked, his faith (the gift from Jesus) is credited as righteousness" (NIV). As an enlightening exercise, compare the KJV and NIV versions of Galatians 2:16. Caleb highlights how the KJV accurately translates that we are justified by **"the faith of Jesus,"** which is His gift to us. (Thank you, Caleb, for highlighting these distinctions.)

There is much more to explore here, but we will have to save it for later. Right now, I simply want to celebrate with those who have acknowledged that we have died to sin and have been raised to a heavenly place in Christ. We have moved from a covenant that ensured death, to one that guarantees life, both in the present and in the ages to come.

With that being said, I pray that we can now progress together, even if our views on the path to paradise differ a bit. The crucial aspect of this journey is understanding that Jesus is with us every step of the way, and He has guaranteed the end result. Our comprehensive knowledge of the entire process, or the lack thereof, will not impact the wonderful outcome He has planned for us as believers.

My next task is to provide you with my best understanding of the number of future resurrections and an overview of the individuals involved in each. The third and final resurrection will be the central focus of this book. While a third resurrection might sound improbable at first to some, let us collectively examine the substantial evidence for it in His Word.

Before we conclude this chapter, I would like to share another thought - my belief that God likely has a much bigger motorcycle than the one I once owned. Perhaps, it can even fly. Moreover, He can probably take us to places far more stunning than the Texas Hill Country, no matter how beautifully He crafted it.

But despite owning these things, He might not be all that interested in material possessions, like bigger bikes, even though His ownership of everything is truly impressive. I believe His primary interest lies in a very personal relationship with each of us. Perhaps, that should be our main focus as well - on our relationship with Him. I imagine He appreciates it when we hold on to Him tightly and sing to Him during the ride of our lives.

3

A Cord of Three Strands

ECCLESIASTES 4:12 ASSERTS that a threefold cord is not easily broken. Considering this, I will illustrate how the writings of John, Moses, and Paul are three strands tightly woven together in "one accord" (an attempt at cleverness). We will begin with John, who harmonizes alongside Moses, and Paul in one beautiful chord (one last attempt).

Indeed, we have touched upon some significant verses from John's writings earlier. However, for a remarkably clear depiction of three distinct harvests, or resurrections, the 14th chapter of Revelation stands out. In Revelation 14:1-5, we encounter the first group of resurrected individuals:

> **"Then I looked**, and lo, on Mount Zion stood the Lamb, and with Him 144,000 who had His name and His Father's name written on their foreheads. And I heard a voice from heaven like the sound of many waters and like the sound of loud thunder; the voice I heard was like the sound of harpers playing on their harps, and they sang a new song... No one could learn that song except the hundred and forty-four thousand who had been redeemed from the earth... these have been redeemed from mankind as **first-fruits** for God and the Lamb, and in their mouth no lie was found, for they are spotless" (Nestle-Aland).

These are the "souls" referred to by John in Revelation 20:4-6, and the evidence supporting this reference follows. Recall that these individuals were those "who had been beheaded... They had not worshipped the beast or his image and had not received the mark on their foreheads or their hands" (NIV). Remember how they "came to life and reigned with Christ for a thousand years." Designated as "blessed and holy," they were active participants in the "first resurrection." John, or rather, the Holy Spirit through John, provides unequivocal clarity. A specific group of humanity, known as "first-fruits," experiences a renewed existence in the context of the "first resurrection."

This initial group was also referenced in Revelation 7:3-4, where the identical "144,000" were bestowed with "a seal on the foreheads." In those times, seals were employed to designate a person's belongings. Given that this group was identified as the "servants of our God" in the same verse, a mark was affixed to their foreheads, signifying their belonging to Him— they were indeed His possession.

Revelation chapter 3, verses 8 and 12, validate the significance of this seal. In those verses, God assures those who "have kept my word and not denied my name" (NIV) that He will "write on him. . . my own new name" (Nestle-Aland). He characterizes individuals within this group as those who overcome.

In Revelation 20:4, we also learn that this identical group did not bear the mark or seal of the beast on their foreheads or hands. Instead, they possessed a distinct seal, granted to them "because of their testimony for Jesus and because of the word of God" (NIV).

Revelation 14:1 affirms the same seal, stating, "His name and His Father's name [were] written on their foreheads" (KJV). As evident from the verses in Revelation found in chapters 3, 7, 14, and 20, they collectively refer to the same group of individuals. These people bore the identical mark on their foreheads and were described as being "redeemed from mankind as first-fruits," actively participating in the "first resurrection."

The Expositor's Greek Testament characterizes this group as "the vanguard who had borne the brunt of the struggle," anticipating a distinct and elevated joy in the ages to come. This commentator further links Revelation 7:1-8, 14:1, and 20:4-6 to this specific group of believers. Other commentators also acknowledge the relevance of these encouraging words to the initial group, recognizing the enduring hardships faced by many throughout the Christian era. Particularly during the formative days of the church, numerous individuals encountered severe trials and endured significant persecution, with some even sacrificing their lives for the sake of the gospel.

I believe our Father, communicating through John, was encouraging these overcomers to stand resolute in "their testimony for Jesus." In return for their steadfastness, they were promised the privilege of ruling and reigning with Him in a future age. If a fellow brother or sister in Christ were to make such a profound sacrifice, I am confident the entire spiritual family would rejoice wholeheartedly for them in their calling, recognizing this extraordinary distinction.

Before diving into a discussion of the second group, it is worth noting how God draws parallels between these resurrection events and harvests of crops. This theme recurs throughout the scriptures, especially in the writings of the three individuals under examination. It adopts an agricultural motif, likening humanity to crops awaiting harvest.

As author Julie Ferwerda asked when she opened the chapter, The Great Harvests, in her book, Raising Hell:

> "Have you ever noticed that the Bible is blooming full of agricultural terms? There's a significant reason for this that goes beyond a nice little farming theme. Consider the frequency of some of these words as they occur in the original languages (Hebrew and Greek): Season – 334; Field – 332; Seed – 300; Crop/Produce – 124; Vineyard – 115; Harvest – 78; Planting – 66; Wheat 45; Barley – 36; Farmer – 26; Grapes – 22; Winepress – 21."

I strongly agree with Julie's statement later in that chapter, emphasizing that we miss out when we fail to dig deep enough into understanding these agricultural references. Following her advice, we will dig a little deeper as we progress further.

In the initial segment of Revelation 14, we observe that God's plan for the harvests commences with the redemption of the first group as "first-fruits" from the earth. Given that they are the first to be harvested, and that John designates them as participants in the first resurrection, it logically follows that a subsequent harvest would be regarded as the second one, pointing to a second resurrection. In verses 14-16, we encounter this second harvest:

> "**Then I looked**, and lo, a white cloud, and seated on the cloud one like the son of man, with a golden crown on his head, and a sharp sickle in his hand. And another angel came out of the temple, calling with a loud voice to him who sat upon the cloud, 'Put in your sickle, and reap, for the hour to reap has come, for the harvest of the earth is fully ripe.' So he who sat upon the cloud swung his sickle on the earth, and the earth was reaped" (Nestle-Aland).

Take note of how the harvest in the earth aligns with the ripeness mentioned in our passage from John 5:28-29. Recall that "the hour" arrives when all those in the tomb will hear His voice and experience either a "resurrection of life" or a "resurrection of judgment." The time for the second harvest has come. It's worth mentioning that preceding the second resurrection, chapter 14, verse 6 reveals that another angel had proclaimed the gospel to "every nation, and kindred, and tongue, and people" (KJV). In essence, this indicates that the earth was ripe and ready for harvesting.

In Revelation 20:12-15, we gain further insight into the concept of being resurrected to life or judgment: "And if anyone's name was not found written in the book of life, he was thrown into the lake of fire" (RSV). Once again, the Holy Spirit through John leaves no room for ambiguity regarding this second resurrection. If there's been any aspect "hidden" in His Word, it has indeed been "hidden in plain sight."

Now, we arrive at what I consider the most astonishing aspect of this entire discussion – another harvest – the third resurrection. Having been informed of a first resurrection, followed by another as the second, it logically follows that the subsequent one is the third harvest – the third resurrection. In verses 18-20 of chapter 14, we read:

> "**Then** another angel came out from the altar, the angel who has power over fire, and he called with a loud voice to him who had the sickle, 'Put in your sickle, and gather the clusters of the vine from the earth, for its grapes are ripe.' So the angel swung his sickle on the earth and gathered the vintage of the earth, and threw it into the great wine press of the wrath of God; and the wine was trodden outside the city,

and blood flowed from the winepress, as high as the horse's bridle, for one thousand six hundred stadia" (Nestle-Aland).

In this metaphorical language, grapes are harvested and transformed by God's wrath in a winepress. We will examine the topic of His wrath later, and you may be surprised to discover what it is and what it accomplishes. Moreover, it is essential to recognize that in the production of wine by the Jewish people, the grapes went through a process called "treading," wherein they were positioned under the feet of the winemaker. This technique entailed **separating the outer flesh of the grape** from the valuable contents within. Paul will also make a reference to this process when we hear his perspective on the three resurrections.

In this passage from Revelation, we also discover that the winepress is situated "outside the city." The question arises: What city? Additionally, we observe blood from the winepress flowing across a distance that scholars have identified as the length of the nation of Israel. When considering our Lord's statement about a man's enemies being those of his own household, we witness a profusion of blood coursing abundantly through the land of His enemies – those who rejected and crucified Him. Here, that blood is metaphorically transformed into wine.

Blood and wine – does this combination sound familiar? And pay attention to the messenger from God emerging from the altar, wielding power over fire. Who was this messenger, and why is it mentioned that he had power over fire? What fire?

Answers to these questions will be addressed later. At this point, beyond merely provoking contemplation, the primary objective is to emphasize how the scriptures allude to a third group destined to be harvested and resurrected. They are referred to as grapes, and they are sent to a winepress and turned into wine.

Next, we will discuss how the count from Moses was in perfect harmony with John's count of three. It is far from coincidental that Israel observed three significant feasts annually, each coinciding with the harvest of three distinct crops. Moses documented these well-known celebrations, named the Feasts of Passover, Pentecost, and Tabernacles (Exodus 23:14-17). That last one, the Feast of Tabernacles, was also referred to as the Feast of Booths, or Succoth.

Three times a year, men were mandated to "appear before the Sovereign Lord" and "celebrate a festival to me" (NIV). These festivals corresponded to three annual holiday pilgrimages to the location of the Tabernacle. Attendance was compulsory for all.

The initial celebration was the Feast of Passover, marking the harvest of barley. This festival took place on the 14th day of the first month in the Jewish calendar, Nissan. This date aligns with our Gregorian calendar, falling between late March and early April.

On the initial day of Passover, typically a Friday, a meal was served in commemoration of Israel's exodus from Egypt. The next day, the Sabbath, marked the commencement of the seven-day Feast of Unleavened Bread. During this period, the first fruits of the barley harvest were presented at the Temple. On the morning following the Sabbath, which was the first day of the new week, the priest would wave a sheaf offering of the grain before the Lord on behalf of the people.

Barley was the grain harvested at this time. As a crop, it matured first, and in Leviticus, we learn that the "first-fruit" of the barley was "mixed with oil," essentially anointed, and then cooked as "an offering by fire to the Lord." Designated as an anointed first-fruit, it was consecrated to the Lord, serving as an earnest or pledge for the complete harvests yet to be gathered throughout the rest of the year.

Moreover, the day the barley offering was presented was termed the Feast of First-fruits, falling on the first day of the new week. The barley squadron seems to symbolize those who mature first in Christ. Recall how Jesus fed the crowds with five loaves of barley? Doesn't that align with the calling of first-fruits, to be a living sacrifice in service to others?

The second obligatory pilgrimage, with its corresponding celebration, was the Feast of Pentecost. Leviticus 23:15-16 specifies that the Israelites were instructed to commence counting fifty days from the Feast of First-fruits to the next feast celebration. Throughout the forty-nine days of this count, known as "the counting of the Omer," the wheat crop was maturing. At the conclusion of the Omer count, the crop was ripe for harvest, and the initial fruits of the wheat could be presented at the Temple for Pentecost. This celebration took place on the 6th of Sivan, corresponding to the first of June on our calendar.

Leviticus 23:17 specifies that two loaves of wheat flour, mixed with leaven, were to be cooked in fire and offered to God at this time. Why two?

Because it represented the second harvest! Additionally, it's noteworthy that both grains, barley and wheat, had to be "cooked" in fire. The description of these feast days is laden with symbolic significance and meaning.

The final celebration was the Feast of Tabernacles, an autumn festival observed on the 15th of Tishrei on the Jewish calendar, typically falling near the end of September to the beginning of October on ours. In Nehemiah 8:1-12, all Israelites and strangers in the land gathered to read the law during this feast. At that moment, they stood together, read it aloud, and collectively proclaimed "Amen," signifying unanimous agreement with God's ways.

While other crops were harvested in late summer and early fall, the attention centered on the grapes for wine. Barley, wheat, and grapes consistently top the list as the three major crops in Israel during that period, according to every historical article I have encountered.

If you explore Jewish customs, you will find that the autumn festivals were associated with greater rejoicing compared to the spring and summer harvests. This heightened joy might be attributed to the fact that the last feast celebrated the harvest of all three crops. Observe the mention of both grain and grapes in Deuteronomy 16:13 – "Another festival, the Feast of Shelters (Tabernacles), must be observed for seven days, after the grain is threshed, and the grapes have been pressed" (Living Bible).

Speaking of celebration and rejoicing, there are a few Hebrew words for feast. "Chag" signifies circling, dancing, or feasting, while "Chagim" (plural) involves celebrations characterized by singing, dancing, and processions in a joyful and festive atmosphere. With all the food and wine, this final celebration must have been an event you would not want to miss. Evidently, our Lord knows how to throw a party.

During the Tabernacles festival, Solomon's Temple was dedicated to the Lord, marking the Israelites' return to Jerusalem for the reconstruction of the Temple following seventy years of Babylonian captivity. Additionally, it was during this celebration that Jesus proclaimed in John 7:37-38, "If anyone is thirsty, let him come to me and drink. He who believes in me, as the Scriptures has said, 'Out of his heart shall flow rivers of living water'" (RSV). Have you observed the subtle connection between water and wine? (More details will follow.)

I appreciate the insights shared by various writers regarding the significance of the seventy bulls offered as sacrifices during this last feast celebration. Specifically, on the first day of Tabernacles, thirteen bulls were sacrificed, followed by twelve on the next day, and continuing in decreasing numbers until seven were offered on the final day. The cumulative total of these sacrifices amounts to seventy bulls.

The number 13 is a number associated with rebellion and mirrors the rebellious 13 tribes of Israel who, despite receiving God's law, struggled to uphold it. In contrast, 7 symbolizes "perfection," while 70 embodies the concept of "completion." This symbolism extends to the span of a man's years and the duration of God's people in captivity. Furthermore, 70 signifies the total number of nations and languages in accordance with Jewish tradition.

When considered collectively, the narrative unfolds: what commenced in rebellion, culminates in perfection, representing the completion of God's plan for humanity and the nations. Tabernacles serves as a prophetic precursor to the liberation from our captivity in sin, emphasizing why God commanded its celebration.

A comprehensive examination of these feast celebrations reveals numerous insights. In essence, Moses highlights the obligation for men to **appear** before God during three major feast celebrations with each commemorating the harvest of three distinct crops at three specific times of the year in three different seasons – Spring, Summer, and Fall. Remarkably, these harvest cycles align perfectly with the three groups earmarked for resurrection, as outlined by John.

Additionally, as we are about to discover, Paul's insights on these events resonate with the same harmonious pattern. It is crucial to emphasize that these alignments are not mere coincidences. In 1st Corinthians chapter 15, beginning in verse 20, Paul wrote:

> "But in fact, Christ **has indeed been raised** from the dead, the first-fruit of those who have fallen asleep. 21. For since death came through a man, the resurrection of the dead comes also through a man. 22. For as in Adam all die, so in Christ all **shall be made alive.** 23. But each one in his own turn: Christ the first-fruits, then, when He comes, those who belong to him. 24. Then the end will come, when He hands over the kingdom to God the Father after he has destroyed all dominion, authority and power. 25. For He

must reign until He has put all enemies under His feet. 26. The last enemy to be destroyed is death. 27. For He has put everything under his feet. Now when it says 'everything' has been put under him, it is clear that this does not include God himself, who put everything under Christ. 28. When he has done this, then the Son himself will be made subject to him who put everything under him, so that God may be all in all" (NIV).

Allow me to draw your attention to several key facts that significantly influence our interpretation of these verses. First, in verse 20, Paul explicitly declares that Christ is the first-fruit of those who have fallen asleep, establishing Him as the initial figure to undergo resurrection. Furthermore, the verb "raised" in the expression "has indeed been raised" is in the perfect tense. This tense choice by Paul explicitly communicates that Jesus had already experienced resurrection.

However, as Paul transitions to discussing the future resurrection of others, he shifts the verb tense to the future with "shall be made alive." Having established Christ as the initial participant in resurrection, Paul proceeds to elaborate on the future vivification, or being "made alive," of all humanity.

In verses 21 and 22, he underscores the idea that just as one man introduced death into the world, another man will bring life to the same collective. Regardless of one's stance on universal salvation, eternal conscious torment, or the annihilation of the wicked, there is a unanimous acknowledgment that all individuals will be "made alive." After all, the judgment and sentencing to salvation, torment, or annihilation, presupposes a return from the state of death, so all can be judged.

Verse 23 introduces the concept of everyone being raised in a specific "turn." The Greek word in this context is "tagma," a military term denoting a company, squadron, or group. According to Strong's Concordance, it suggests an arrangement in a precise sequence, indicating meticulous planning. Given that all are in Christ, and considering that He was raised, the metaphorical use of "tagma" implies an organized grouping of people in squadrons who will also be made alive.

This metaphor is further explained in the subsequent portion of verse 23 and extends into verse 24. The crucial point that Paul emphasizes here bears repeating: because we are all "in" Adam, and he experienced death, we are all destined for the same fate. However, by the same logic, we are all also "in" Christ, and since He underwent resurrection, we are all destined for resurrection to life. This idea is reiterated in verse 21 when Paul restates that death came through one man to all, but resurrection to life for all comes through another.

Based on the information presented here, a correction is necessary for the standard translation commonly found in many Bibles. The initial group in the list to be made alive in the future, is rendered "Christ the first-fruits," as we just observed in our NIV translation. However, it cannot pertain to Him for several reasons.

First, the expression "shall be made alive" is written in the future tense, and given that Jesus had already risen at the time of this writing, it cannot be in reference to Him. Second, the noun introduced in the sentence, "tagma," denotes a group, rather than an individual. This point is substantiated by Revelation 20:4-6, which reveals a group of people, or squadron, being "made alive" as participants in the first resurrection. It is beneficial to revisit this passage to firmly grasp the identity of those in the inaugural squadron:

> "And I saw the souls of those who had been beheaded
> because of their testimony for Jesus and the word of God.
> They did not worship the beast or its image and had not
> received its mark on their foreheads or hands. They came
> to life and reigned with Christ for a thousand years." (The
> rest of the dead did not come to life until the thousand years
> were ended.) This is the first resurrection" (NIV).

Third, it is also essential to note the absence of an article preceding the word "christos" in the initial segment of verse 23, when naming the first group to be raised in the future. Other scholars have pointed out that we are not compelled to automatically infer the term "Christ" from "christos," without an article preceding it. Allow me to elaborate.

In the Greek, "christos" means "anointed." When you add an article in front of it, you get "the anointed" or "Christ," as seen in the preceding verse 22 and in the latter part of verse 23. In both of those instances, an article precedes "christos." However, in the middle occurrence, when naming the first group to be raised, "christos" appears without an article, setting it apart from the other two instances. Consequently, a more accurate translation of this phrase would be "anointed first-fruit."

Taking into consideration all the points presented above, we can infer that this language is directed towards a group who are "in Him" and part of the "first resurrection." Despite Jesus being the first individual to experience resurrection, He is not in Himself, and He does not represent the initial squadron to be raised in the future. Jesus played the role of a trailblazer, paving the way for all the groups that are in Him to be made alive, as He already has been.

This interpretation aligns more coherently than the idea of a significant announcement about squadrons to be "made alive," only to find one man, and then everyone else, as is typically conveyed by the poor translation we find in most Bibles. Consequently, the initial group in Christ to be resurrected, or "made alive," is identified as the "anointed first-fruit."

First-fruit was the term also employed by John in Revelation 14:4. This group is the first to be harvested among all believers, with a second squadron, comprising those who belong to Christ at His coming, following suit. The NIV categorizes this second group as "those who belong to Him" at the time of His appearance, distinguishing them from those who do not.

Personally, I find a more accurate translation designates the second group as "those who are Christ's in His presence," as rendered by the Concordant Literal. Considering the second group, let us recall the words of Jesus in John 11:25 (RSV): "I am the resurrection and the life; he who believes in me, though he die, yet shall he live, and whoever lives" (after they are resurrected) "and believes in me shall never die" (put on immortality, not participating in the second death).

After the harvest of the initial two groups, verse 24 clarifies that the culmination follows, wherein He delivers the kingdom to God the Father. Some interpret this as the definitive endpoint. According to this perspective, the doomsday clock has rung for those who did not believe in Jesus before their death. The majority, it is argued, will face eternal torment or annihilation in the lake of fire, while the minority in the second group will ascend to heaven and unite with the first group for eternity.

However, the main subject of our text is the order of squadrons destined to be "made alive," not dead, as our Father is declared to be the "God of the living, not the dead" (Matthew 22:32, NLT). The central theme of this passage in Corinthians revolves around squadrons to be made alive, not "time." The Greek word employed for "end" in this context is "telos." According to the BAGD (a Greek-English lexicon), "telos" denotes "the goal toward which **a movement** is being directed, end, goal, outcome." This definition is supported by Strongs Concordance, which indicates that the word signifies "the principal end, aim, purpose."

The initial word in verse 24, "Then," serves as another clue to what Paul is addressing. "Then" signifies "a particle of succession." Succession to what? The answer is evident: Succession to the list of squadrons destined to be "made alive"—the central theme that Paul is addressing in these verses.

The essence of this passage revolves around the "goal, movement being directed, outcome, aim, and purpose" concerning the order in which men are to be made alive. Given that the subject involves groups, with Paul explicitly mentioning two, it follows that "the end" naturally alludes to the conclusion or culmination of these groups. Considering the context, the likelihood of it being a reference to "time" appears notably weak, especially when we also take into account the insights provided by John and Moses—both emphasizing three groups of crops to be harvested.

Applying straightforward logic, some interpreters translate the phrase "Then the end will come," as "Then comes the remainder." In either case, I interpret this expression as alluding to the conclusion of the sequence of squadrons of men to be "made alive." Within this context, we encounter the last group to be vivified—the third harvest, which represents the ultimate aim and final outcome in this ordered sequence.

To help identify this concluding group, Paul introduces the idea: "For he must reign until he puts all enemies under His feet." This theme of enemies being placed "under His feet" is reiterated several times in the closing verses of our Corinthians text, culminating in verse 28 with the proclamation "that God may be all in all." This pivotal triumph signifies the moment when death is obliterated, as found in verse 26.

A pertinent question arises: Why does Paul employ the phrase "under His feet" five times in three verses, 25-28? The answer lies in the Holy Spirit's reference to the grapes, who undergo the winepress of His wrath and are placed "under His feet," outside the city.

We will cover many other important details in the coming chapters, but for now, I would like us to remember the order of events.

1. The first and second resurrections occur, then afterwards, some are placed in a lake of fire. That immersion is called the second death.
2. A third resurrection can only mean there are people lifted out of that same lake from death to life.
3. After those from the third group have been raised to life, Paul informs us that death is destroyed and God is all in all.

The following chart may be helpful as it summarizes the three harvests/resurrections.

Scriptural References	First Harvest Resurrection	Second Harvest Resurrection	Third Harvest Resurrection
Revelation Chapter 14	First-fruit	Crops: ripe/ready (His) at the hour of His coming	Grapes thrown into the winepress of God's wrath
Leviticus Chapter 23	Passover: Barley First-fruit	Pentecost: Wheat	Tabernacles: Grapes sent to the winepress
1 Corinthians Chapter 15	First-fruit	His at His coming	Enemies put under His feet (winepress)
John Chapter 5		Ones with good deeds (His) at the hour of His coming	
Revelation Chapter 20		Ones in the Book of Life with good deeds (His)	

Here is another intriguing observation from these scriptures. In Revelation 20:4-6, we discovered that the span between the first and second resurrection is described as "a thousand years." Thanks to the insights of Dr. Kenneth Gentry, I now interpret the thousand years as a figure of speech signifying "a long period of time." It is akin to the expression "cattle on a thousand hills," not meant to be taken literally but conveying the idea of "a bunch of beef." Nevertheless, for those who take the thousand years literally, it still signifies a substantial duration.

Now, let us consider the temporal intervals between the harvests. There were 50 calendar days between the first and second harvests, and 125 days between the second and third. So, if we equate the first 50 days with a thousand years, the subsequent 125 days would represent an even greater extended period.

While we may not have precise knowledge of the exact durations of these periods, one certainty remains: the harvests of the three crops do not occur simultaneously; there are distinct time intervals between them. Consequently, the third resurrection cannot be considered as a part of the second; it is entirely distinct and unfolds at a later time.

Additionally, it is crucial to recognize that the entire harvest season is not concluded until both grains are harvested for bread and the grapes are collected for wine. It seems that God's communion with mankind achieves fullness only when the bread and wine are prepared and served. (We will revisit this crucial theme later.)

This concludes our trio of interconnected harvests. As a parting thought, we share an observation from Julie Ferwerda for your consideration. She highlighted that each crop required a distinct process for removing the unwanted chaff. Barley underwent winnowing, a gentle blowing process, while wheat was threshed, a more robust method. In contrast, grapes were directed to the wine press, the most vigorous process of all, separating the flesh from the byproduct—the juice that transforms into wine.

At this juncture, I feel a compelling urge to commence presenting the numerous instances where these three groups emerge in the scriptures. This revelation has given me a new perspective, providing reasons for several elements in the Bible that previously seemed "odd" to me. They now align and make perfect sense.

As examples of initially perplexing elements, I questioned why individuals began speaking in a foreign language when filled with the Holy Spirit's fire. Similarly, I pondered why Jesus chose to turn water into wine as His first miracle instead of, for instance, healing someone of blindness, or raising someone from the dead, which might seem more impressive. However, it has become clear that the answers to these questions foreshadow some highly significant events in our future.

Additional intriguing questions related to this topic include: Why are there three manifestations of the Godhead? Why did Jesus raise someone from the dead on three separate occasions during His earthly ministry? What is the significance of the three temptations of Christ, and why did Jesus pray three times in the garden before His death?

Why does it specify that Jesus broke the bread into two pieces and then took a cup of wine during the last supper? Additionally, why did He spend three days in the grave, and what significance lies in Paul spending three days in darkness before being filled with the Spirit and healed of his blindness? Lastly, what is the reasoning behind there being three heavens?

I am eager to share my insights on these questions. However, as crucial as these topics are, I sense that several other questions need to be addressed before we can progress together. Acknowledging that a belief in three resurrections may challenge some previously held beliefs, it's important to recognize that this idea did not initially align with my own paradigm. It took years of study and prayer before I began to see it more clearly.

As mentioned earlier, change tends to be challenging for us humans. Resistance to change is a survival instinct, and often, caution is necessary before fully embracing it. At this juncture, I recognize the importance of being respectful to others by addressing some of their concerns before moving forward. Once again, my intention is not to compel you to believe me outright but to encourage you to contemplate the ideas presented in the next few chapters and seek guidance from our Father to discern His message for you.

4

Is a Third Even Possible?

AFTER INTRODUCING THE idea in the last chapter, some may still be questioning the feasibility of a third resurrection, particularly given what they may have learned previously about the lake of fire. In my youth, at the Baptist church I attended, the teaching was that once someone is cast into that lake, there is no possibility of escape. However, after years of study, my perspective has changed. F.H. Robison (1885-1932) once said: "Our concepts of truth are usually colored more or less by teachers," and I submit, there has been a lot of coloring by well-intended but flawed artists. Below are a few items to consider before coloring the lake as a final and eternal destination for all who experience it.

Consider the words "thrown" or "cast" in the phrase, "thrown into the lake of fire," and the word "threw" in the phrase, "threw it (the vintage - grapes) into the great winepress of God's wrath." These terms are translations of the same Greek word, "ballo" (Strong's 906). They both appear in the aorist tense and indicative mood. This tense captures a snapshot of an event, and both the tense and the mood imply an "entry into a phase without any reference to permanency," as explained by the renowned Dr. Daniel Wallace of Dallas Theological Seminary.

There is more to discover regarding the word, "ballo," and its translation as "thrown" or "cast," when other alternatives like "put" or "placed" were available to the translators as well. I intend to explore these word choices in greater detail when we delve into a more comprehensive discussion of the lake of fire in Chapter 6.

Equally important for our reflection, I have discovered over the years that many Christians are not even aware of the controversy surrounding the translation of the Greek word "aion." In its adjective form, "aiwnios" is the sole term used in the New Testament to describe the duration of time spent in judgment in the lake of fire. Having been a member of 13 different churches throughout my lifetime, I observed that eleven of the ministers were either unfamiliar with the topic, or chose not to address it with their congregation. (My wife and I have relocated six times, primarily due to company transfers, with one move for retirement, and the last one to be closer to our grandkids.)

One of the eleven ministers requested that I not even mention the topic to others, as he did not want to "confuse the flock." Other ministers may have different reasons for avoiding the issue, and I am not here to find fault. God understands the challenges involved in leading a large and diverse group of people, many of whom are emotionally tied to previously held beliefs. As we've mentioned, change is difficult, and we must be respectful of that fact. Nevertheless, for this discussion, the controversy is unavoidable.

"Aion" is the Greek noun from which we derive our English words "eon" or "age." I began exploring its meaning in my early teenage years, and I was surprised to discover the various ways it had been translated. I learned that many, perhaps, most of the early Church Fathers in the eastern part of the Roman world during that time, believed the noun meant "age," and the adjective form meant "age-lasting." This caught my attention, because most of these men grew up speaking, reading, and writing the Greek language as their native tongue. Some, like Clement of Alexandria, even taught at a university level with that language.

However, many in the Latin segment of the Church, situated in the western part of the Roman world, believed that it meant "eternal," well, most of the time. Augustine was among them, and his influence extended significantly among Christians in western Europe. What troubled me about him was his expression of "hatred" toward the Greek language. I also came across instances where he and Jerome, the author of the Vulgate, who was proficient in both Greek and Latin, engaged in a few "discussions" about the translation of this term. (That conflict should not be surprising to anyone familiar with church history, acknowledging the diversity of opinions within the Church even today.)

According to church historians, Augustine's opinions came to dominate the thinking in the western religious world. When King James requested

54 scholars of his day to translate the Bible into English, he made a specific request not disrupt the orthodoxy of the Church, much of which had been influenced by Augustine. This was understandable, as leaders in the Church during that time occasionally responded harshly to those with a different understanding of God's Word.

As a result, many of Augustine's ideas influenced the King James translation. Where "eternity" would not make sense, when translating "aion" into English, they opted for different words, such as "world," "never," and "age." Even as a teenager, I knew the Greek word for "world" was "kosmos" and quickly recognized the conflicts. Whom should I believe? I also learned how the controversy has persisted.

As a birthday gift during my teenage years, I received a copy of Young's Analytical Concordance, which I still use. Later, I purchased a Strong's Concordance, and I highly recommend both to any serious student of the Bible. However, concerning the meaning of "aion," Young sided with the Greek-speaking eastern part of the early Church, while Strong's leaned towards the western Latin understanding – well, mostly.

In my opinion, Strong's interpretation of "aion" appears to be imprecise and is notably inconsistent. Strong's definition characterizes "aion" as **"an age; by extension perpetuity,"** a formulation that introduces ambiguity at best, and incongruency at worst. Additionally, the translation choices made by Strong for "aion" include "ever" 71 times, "world" 38 times, "never" 6 times, "evermore" 4 times, "age" 2 times, "eternal" 2 times, and "forever" 5 times.

Initially, I pondered the flexibility of a word that could encompass such a multitude of meanings, leading me to consider it the most versatile term across all human languages. Later, as a mathematics major in college, I encountered a stark contrast: numerical symbols, terms, or numbers in mathematics distinctly represent either the finite or the infinite. In mathematics, the two concepts are inherently distinct and mutually exclusive. Additionally, in my explorations of the Bible, I observed instances where "aions" exhibited both beginnings and endings, as exemplified in 1 Corinthians 10:11. This contradicts the notion of eternity. Consequently, translations like the NIV occasionally render "aion" and "aions" accurately as "age" and "ages," but not consistently either.

Moreover, as a linguistic axiom, the adjective form of a noun inherently cannot surpass the scope of the noun itself. For instance, I receive a "daily" newspaper once a day and a "monthly" bill once per month. Neither can be aptly characterized as everlasting or eternal, even though at times my tax bills seem like they may be forever. Consequently, the question arises: how can an adjective, rooted in the concept of age, be accurately translated as everlasting or eternal?

In summarizing my studies, I have not encountered a single instance where "age," "ages," "age-lasting," "age-during," or "for the age" did not serve as a fitting translation for the singular, plural, adjective, or adverbial forms of "aion." Even when connected to concepts like God, or life, I find no issue with employing one of these forms for translation.

For instance, scholars have observed that characterizing God as the God of this age, the past ages, or the ages to come, in no way constrains His eternalness, just as the phrase "the God of Abraham, Isaac, and Jacob" does not confine Him to be the God of those three only. These expressions are merely emphasizing something special about Him within a specific age or group.

Concerning life, I interpret "aionian life" as simply emphasizing the quality of the life that God has designed for us both in the present and in the ages to come. This is consistent with our previous discussion on the two phases of "being made alive." This perspective has been endorsed by numerous Bible scholars throughout Church history, though it was never addressed in eleven of the churches I attended. The scriptures explicitly affirm that we can experience "aionian life" in the present, even though we will all undergo death, unless alive at His coming. Consequently, it cannot be referencing immortality, but rather a purpose-driven life in Christ in the present.

Additionally, my exploration of the Septuagint revealed that the Hebrew equivalent of "aion" is the term "olam." While many scholars characterize olam as "an unknown period of time, or hidden time," Strong's Concordance holds a divergent view, describing it as "perpetual," despite **multiple instances** where the time period reaches an absolute end!

This raises questions about the accuracy of Strong's Concordance in assessing these two Greek and Hebrew words. Here are three examples: Jonah was in the belly of the whale for "olam" (Jonah 2:6), a slave would serve his master for "olam" (Exodus 21:6), and the Aaronic priesthood was meant to endure for "olam" (Exodus 40:15), and it was eventually replaced by the order of Melchizedek (Hebrews 11:11-12). P.T. Barnum (1810-1891) also cites three additional examples in his writings, where "olam" is used to describe the lifespan of hills, stars, and rainbows. (Yes, the famous circus impresario – he understood the significance of these terms.)

I have identified 31 instances in the Old Testament where olam was used to describe something that was unequivocally not eternal, and twelve instances where it was either doubled, or in a plural form. These examples are inconsistent with the notion that this word inherently conveys a sense of perpetuity or eternity.

Additionally, translating "olam" as "eternity" in the third chapter of Ecclesiastes is equally perplexing to me. In that passage, we encounter words that were melodically conveyed by some birds in my youth, illustrating a time and purpose for everything under heaven (as immortalized in the song "Turn! Turn! Turn!" by The Byrds, 1965). Our translators, some of whom believed that olam meant eternity, rendered verse 11 in this way: "He has put eternity (or 'world' in the KJV) into man's mind, yet so that he cannot find out what God has done from the beginning to the end" (RSV).

This phrasing raises questions. Why would God place eternity in our minds, and for what purpose, especially if it was meant to be unknowable? However, the idea that God would implant something in our intellects to remain elusive becomes clearer once we understand that "olam" refers to an unknown or hidden period of time. With this understanding, we find more comforting words that make perfect sense to me and others.

Right after enumerating twenty-eight different times in our lives, the passage conveys that, despite our awareness and experience of these events, the specific timing remains concealed from our understanding, our intellect. No one knows when they will begin or end, except our Father in heaven. The subsequent comforting thought is that, although the timing eludes us, it is known to Him. Each event has been intricately designed and orchestrated by Him with a specific purpose in mind. Consequently, we can find profound comfort in the knowledge that He is aware. **He knows**, and verse 11 summarizes where: "He has made everything beautiful in His time" (RSV). That is truly awe-inspiring!

I could delve extensively into the issue of translating "aion" and "olam" as terms for eternity, but it might be more enlightening to consider the research conducted by Dr. David Konstan, during his tenure at Brown

University, and Dr. Ilarri Ramali, affiliated with the Università Cattolica di Milano. Collaboratively, they authored a book titled "Terms for Eternity." In essence, their research explores how the adjective form of "aion" was employed before, during, and after the period when the Bible was written, shedding light on the Greek understanding both within and outside of biblical contexts. The excerpt below is derived from their book and was graciously shared by David for inclusion in this book.

> "Apart from the Platonic philosophical vocabulary, which is specific to only a few authors, aiônios does not mean "eternal"; it acquires this meaning only when it referred to God, and only because the notion of eternity was included in the conception of God: for the rest, it has a wide range of meanings and its possible renderings are multiple, but it does not mean "eternal." In particular, when it is associated with life or punishment, it denotes their belonging to the world or age to come. Another term, aidios, which always meant "eternal" in the strict sense, according to Jews, Greeks, early Christians, and the Bible, referred exclusively to future life and bliss, but never to future punishment, fire, and the like when applied to mankind."

Note: David's expertise lies in ancient Greek and Latin literature, and he has served as a professor of Classics at NYU following three decades at Brown, where he holds the title of John Rowe Workman Distinguished Professor Emeritus of Classics and Professor Emeritus of Comparative Literature. Having met David and attended one of his lectures, I discovered him to be a person who embodies kindness by sharing his strength rather than highlighting others' weaknesses.

In private discussions with him, it appears that David may lean towards the interpretation that "aiônios" does not denote eternity, even in reference to God. Another acquaintance, Dr. Thomas Talbott, has a different view, and posits that the meaning of the adjective is intimately connected to the noun it modifies, suggesting that the term may signify eternity when describing God. James Hollandsworth, the Baptist minister mentioned earlier, provided a comprehensive summary of these terms in the appendix of his book, "The Savior of All Men," aligning with my understanding that it never meant "eternity."

In summary, I am appreciative of the insights offered by these men and women of God and the chance to share that quote from Ilarri's and David's research. Later in this book, I will also reference some of Tom's insights from his great book, "The Inescapable Love of God."

Considering there is another resurrection well beyond the second, and acknowledging the controversy surrounding the translation of "aion," perhaps the door has been opened a little more for a new understanding of God's plan concerning the lake of fire. Yet, some may inquire: "What about the scriptures describing a place 'where their worm dieth not, and their fire is not quenched' (Mark 9:48)? What about God's justice? What about His wrath?" These are pertinent questions, and addressing them will be the focus of the next chapter.

5

God's Wrath, Righteousness/Justice

I WILL START this chapter by referring to the work of Santo Calarco, D.D., who has served as a pastor in Australia since 1981. In his book, "Amazed By Grace," he shares some enlightening perspectives on God's justice and wrath. I wholeheartedly recommend it as one of the most thought-provoking books I have ever read.

Santo initiated a discussion on God's wrath by utilizing a passage from the first chapter of Isaiah. In that passage, God imparts valuable insights into His personality and thought processes. The words were specifically directed at Judah and Jerusalem, and I am firmly convinced that God intended for the rest of the nations throughout history to glean knowledge about His nature and attributes through His interactions with them. Here are some excerpts from that chapter:

> 4. Ah, sinful nation, a people loaded with guilt, a brood of evil doers, children given to corruption! They have forsaken the Lord; they have spurned the Holy One of Israel and turned their backs on Him. . . 21. See how the faithful city has become a harlot! She was once full of justice; righteousness used to dwell in her – but now murderers! 22. Your silver has become dross; your choice of wine has become diluted with water. 23. Your rulers are rebels, companions of thieves; they all love bribes and chase

after gifts. They do not defend the cause of the fatherless; the widow's case does not come before them. 24. Therefore, the Lord, the Lord Almighty, the Mighty One of Israel, declares: '**Ah, I will get relief from my foes and avenge myself on my enemies. 25. I will turn my hand against you. . .**' (NIV).

Before proceeding, let us take a moment to address this question posed by Santo: What do you think God will do in His righteous anger and wrath to get relief and revenge when He turns against His enemies – His foes – those that rejected and stood against Him? Take a moment or two to reflect on it before reading God's response in the remainder of verse 25.

While pondering this question, let me give you an answer provided by James and John. A close friend of mine and I discovered it several years ago while reviewing the 9th chapter of Luke. In that account, we discovered that Jesus was passing through Samaria for the second time on a journey back to Jerusalem. The initial visit was documented in John 4, where Jesus spent two days witnessing and leading many to believe that He was the Messiah.

Before returning for the second time, Jesus dispatched messengers to prepare the people for His imminent return. Despite this, a considerable number chose not to believe Him, and consequently, they rejected the message that He was their Messiah. This occurred prior to His second coming. Does this narrative sound familiar?

Upon learning about the rejection, James and John, two gentlemen that were in a close relationship with Jesus, and had come along for the second trip, hastily inquired of Him whether they should summon fire down from heaven to consume these unbelievers. I guess they thought burning unbelievers in literal fire would be in sync with His plan. However, Jesus turned and rebuked them. Evidently, their idea was off the mark. Perhaps, this type of action had never entered our Lord's thoughts, especially given His mission to save the world, not judge it.

With the above in mind, let us now look at the correct response to Santo's question, per a quote from God Himself found in the remainder of verse 25 in our Isaiah passage: "I will turn my hand against you, **I will thoroughly purge away your dross and remove all your impurities**" (NIV). The New Century Version translates this verse as: "I will turn against you and cleanse away all your wrongs as if with soap; I will extract all the worthless things from you."

Santo asks: "Was that the answer you were expecting – that God's retribution, revenge, and wrath is the eradication of evil from within?" It is certainly in keeping with Hosea 14:4, where God said of Israel: "I will heal their faithlessness; I will love them freely, for my anger has turned from them" (RSV).

This is also aligning with what John said when he first laid his eyes upon Jesus: "Behold the Lamb of God which taketh away the sin of the world" (John 1:29, KJV). The Greek word translated as "taketh," according to Strong's, means "to remove," just as in our Isaiah passage. Perhaps this is why Jesus asserted in Matthew 21:31 that tax collectors and harlots enter the Kingdom of God **ahead** of His adversaries, including those within His own household, Israel. Notice: The ones who rejected Him come in last, but they do come in! The only conceivable way for this to occur is through a comprehensive purging and the elimination of their impurities. It seems comparable to grapes entering the winepress of His wrath.

Santo highlights another passage that provides further insight into the nature and character of our Father. This passage is extracted from Chapter 1 of Zephaniah:

> "14. The great day of the Lord is near – near and coming quickly. Listen! The cry on the day of the Lord will be bitter, the shouting of the warrior there. 15. That day will be a day of wrath, a day of distress and anguish, a day of trouble and ruin, a day of darkness and gloom, a day of clouds and blackness, 16. a day of trumpet and battle cry against the fortified cities and against the corner towers. 17. I will bring distress on the people and they will walk like blind men because they have sinned against the Lord. Their blood will be poured out like dust and their entrails like filth. 18. Neither their silver or their gold will be able to save them on the day of the Lord's wrath. **In the fire of His jealousy** the whole world will be consumed, for He will make a sudden end of all who live on earth" (NIV).

As Santo emphasizes, the language used is highly graphic. However, he observes another crucial point: the Lord's wrath is intricately linked to the fire of His jealousy. This theme of gathering nations for judgment persists, continuing in Chapter 3, Verse 8.

> "Therefore wait for Me, says the Lord, for the day I will stand up to testify. I have decided to assemble the nations, to gather the kingdoms and pour out my wrath upon them – all my fierce anger. The whole world will be consumed by the fire of My jealous anger. 9. **Then I will purify the lips of the peoples**, that all of them may call on the name of the Lord and serve Him shoulder to shoulder" (NIV).

What exactly is "the fire of My jealous anger"? Santo answers with a quote from Solomon in the Song of Songs from chapter 8: verse 6:

> "Place me like a seal over your heart, like a seal on your arm; for love is as strong as death, its jealousy unyielding as the grave. It burns like a blazing fire, like a mighty flame. 7. Many waters cannot quench love; rivers cannot wash it away" (NIV).

Santo continues: "Wrath and judgment are expressions of God's possessive, jealous love. It is so passionate that it is often expressed using violet language and imagery! Fire is a symbol of the unyielding jealousy of a God that refuses to give up on those He desires; a fiery love that cannot be quenched." I will add that 1 Corinthians 13: 7-8 informs us that love endures all things, is not easily angered, always hopes, always perseveres, and never fails. Since God is love, this is a description of who He is. This is how He loves, and He does so, eternally. The fire of His jealous anger cannot be quenched! It purifies the lips of the people and causes them to call upon Him and serve Him shoulder to shoulder!

I can almost anticipate objections with this question: "But what about God's sense of justice? What about Judgment Day?" Before providing an answer, it is crucial to recognize that "justice" and "righteousness" stem from the same Hebrew word, tsadaq. The equivalence extends to the Greek language, where the term dikaios can be translated as either justice or righteousness. This implies that God's justice and His righteousness are inherently synonymous.

This also implies that the portrayal of God by translators can significantly differ based on their perspectives. Once the reader grasps this reality, God brings us back to that same beautiful place where we are compelled to answer the question: "Who do you say I am?"

In his book, Santo gives his perspective and enlightens us about the Hebrew root word for justice/righteousness, which signifies "to be in correct working order." Leviticus 19:36 mandates, you shall have just weights and balances. The Complete Word Study Old Testament further defines the same word, 6663 in Strong's, as "to be (make) right – to cleanse or clear."

However, as Christopher Marshall explained in Calarco's book, when we contemplate righteousness, our English minds often narrowly perceive it as a manifestation of private ethical purity. Meanwhile, justice is typically associated with our legal sense of fairness in a public court of law. Yet, there is another dimension to God's righteousness/justice that warrants further consideration. It involves restoring things to working order, making things right, cleansing, and clearing—essentially, the process of restoration. This constitutes the essence of God's righteousness and justice.

For instance, Romans 1:15-17 characterizes the Gospel that brings salvation as the righteousness/justice of God. Marshall highlights that these attributes are often overlooked, as Western minds are preoccupied with contemplating God's moral purity and how He ensures that wrongdoers receive their just consequences.

I believe God provided Santo with another compelling example, as conveyed in chapter three in his book. He shares the story of his friend Tony, a mechanical engineer tasked with overseeing petrol pumps in the Australian bush to guarantee they were just. If any pump was found to be unjust, Tony was responsible for making the necessary repairs. Consequently, Tony was referred to as a "Justifier."

His responsibility was not to justify himself, as he was already highly qualified and had demonstrated his capability for doing the job. His role was to justify the objects he was working on. When Tony identifies as a Justifier, he isn't boasting about his moral purity, although he may indeed be an upstanding person. Instead, he is simply conveying the essence of his job—repairing petrol pumps.

Likewise, God serves as our "mechanical engineer," fully capable of justifying us. When He speaks of His justice/righteousness, He isn't boasting about His ethical purity, as we are already aware of that. Rather, He is revealing aspects of His personality, providing insights into His nature. God delights in repairing and restoring, and He excels at it! Romans 4:5 affirms that He is the justifier of the ungodly—those who are not in good working condition.

Pause for a moment and contemplate the distinction between God's concept of justice and ours, particularly in the context of murder. Our human understanding deems justice served when the offender is apprehended, convicted, sentenced, and incarcerated, or even subjected to the death penalty. This represents the extent of our capabilities, as our concept of justice is inherently limited.

However, God possesses the capacity and inclination to accomplish far more than our imagination allows. First, He can and will resurrect the one taken from us, thereby bestowing eternal blessings, and restoring relationships that were temporarily lost in this life. Furthermore, after fixing and correcting that side of the justice equation better than it was before, on the other side of that same equation, He can eventually bring the convicted one to genuine repentance. Subsequently, He holds the ability to justify that person—renewing by clearing, cleansing, and certifying that the individual is reinstated to good working condition. This mirrors the transformative experiences of individuals like David and Paul, both of whom were involved in the death of others.

Due to our limitations, mankind often perceives justice through the lens of a strict "under the law" mindset, adhering to the old principles of "eye for an eye" and "payback" justice. However, since Jesus has paid for our sins, Paul was able to declare, "But now the righteousness of God apart from the law has been made known, to which the Law and the Prophets testify" (Romans 3:21, NIV). Israel was the sole nation placed "under the Law" for their training, and subsequently, for ours through their testimony. God's law functioned as a mirror, revealing to them their sins and their inability to adhere to it.

Aren't we Gentiles in the same condition? Under the same law, we would all face condemnation. However, under the new justice system of Grace, He chose to rectify the situation by settling our debts, permanently restoring and reshaping us in His image and likeness. This has been His intention from the very beginning.

Observe how this fresh system of justice, which is Grace, was witnessed by the Law and the Prophets. God's unchanging character and fervor for shaping us into His likeness persist until He brings us to completion. His will shall prevail on earth, as it already is in heaven, and this seemingly impossible task will be accomplished when His justice/righteousness rectifies both sides of the equation.

This is why Professor G.E. Ladd clarifies that righteousness is primarily about "a relationship rather than an ethical quality... Essentially, 'righteousness' is a concept of relationship... It isn't merely a term denoting personal ethical character but signifies faithfulness to a relationship."

Recall how the initial phase of "being made alive" revolves around a relationship. Santo: "Justice-righteousness focuses on relationships. God is shown to keep His covenant and maintain relationships and this in the face of very bad human behavior! Nehemiah 9:33 (NIV) – 'In all that has happened to us, you have remained righteous (tsadaq); you have acted faithfully, while we acted wickedly'... He keeps His word regardless of our behavior. Justice in the Bible is about God, the judge, intervening to rescue, save and deliver."

Below are a few scriptures that verify what Santo was writing about:

Isaiah 51:5 – "My righteousness draws near speedily, my salvation is on the way, and my arm will bring justice to the nations" (NIV).

Psalm 71:2 – "Rescue me and deliver me in your righteousness; turn your ear to me and save me" (NIV).

Isaiah 30:18 – "Yet the Lord longs to be gracious to you; therefore, he rises to show you compassion. For (because) the Lord is a God of justice" (NIV).

Romans 3:23,24 – "for all have sinned and fall short of the glory of God, and are justified freely by His grace through the redemption that came by Christ Jesus" (NIV).

Matthew 12:17-21 – "This was to fulfill what was spoken through the prophet Isaiah (Jesus had just healed a large group of people): 'Here is my servant whom I have chosen, the one I love, in whom I delight; I will put my Spirit on Him, and he will proclaim justice (Strong's - a decision, judgment, by implication - justice) to the nations. He will not quarrel or cry out; no one will hear his voice in the streets. A bruised reed he will not break, and a smoldering wick he will not snuff out, till he leads (from the treasury of His heart – see verse 35) justice (His form of justice) to (complete) victory. In his name the nations will put their hope" (NIV).

It is evident: God's passionate love, patience, gentleness, kindness, and unwavering determination emerge victorious. His relationship with us remains constant; His love is inescapable, and His justice/righteousness is unstoppable. Together, they usher in salvation, rescue, deliverance, graciousness, compassion, healing, and hope. All these promises flow directly from the treasure chest of His heart; they are highly valued by Him, and He ardently desires to bestow them upon us.

The day will come when the awareness of His passions—His goodness—will humble humanity as we experience the richness of His grace and kindness far surpassing our expectations as previously discussed in Ephesians 2:7 (KJV) – "That in the ages (aions) to come (the future), He will show (that means we must not understand it completely now, or He would not have to show us) the exceeding richness of his grace in his kindness (it will exceed our current expectations) towards us through Christ Jesus."

What about His judgments, though? I mean, God's judgments are genuinely frightening, aren't they? Even the disciple "whom Jesus loved" issued a solemn warning: "And they shall come forth; they that have done good, unto the resurrection of life, and they that have done evil, unto the resurrection of damnation" (John 5:29, KJV).

Certainly, I acknowledge the concern. However, to initiate this discussion, we must address another issue related to the translation of a specific word found in the King James text we just quoted. "Damnation" is a term associated with the lake of fire. It was coined by a Latin lawyer named Tertullian, who lived about two hundred years after the time of Christ.

When you search for "damnation" in the KJV, you will encounter it eleven times. However, there is no equivalent word in the vocabulary of the Greek New Testament that specifically means "damnation." In all eleven instances, the Greek word underlying "damnation" is either krima (2917) or krisis (2920). Both words convey the fundamental concept of rendering a decision or judgment.

Out of the seventy-five instances where krima or krisis were used, only eleven were selected to be translated as "damnation" in the KJV. Rendering the other sixty-four instances with the term "damnation" would result in nonsensical sentences. However, translating all of them with the idea of a decision or judgment being made, makes perfect sense. Therefore, a more precise translation of the last part of John 5:29 should read: "and they that have done evil, unto a resurrection of judgment," not damnation.

The next focal point of our discussion is how we perceive His judgments. As an illustrative example, let us review the following passage in Isaiah, where we encounter God's judgment and gain further insights into His personality.

> Isaiah 66:22-24: "For as the new heavens and the new earth which I will make shall remain before me, says the LORD, so shall your descendants and your name remain. From new moon to new moon, and from Sabbath to Sabbath, **all flesh** shall come to worship before me, says the LORD. And they shall go forth and look on the dead bodies of the men who have rebelled against me; for **their worm** shall not die, **their fire** shall not be quenched, and they shall be an abhorrence to **all flesh**" (RSV).

First, the language being used here is metaphorical. This symbolic rhetoric was familiar language to the Hebrews. Consider, for instance, when Saul died and David ascended the throne. In 2 Samuel 22:8 (NIV), David proclaimed, "The earth trembled and quaked; the foundations of heaven shook." While this description may not have been a literal seismic event, it symbolized a real transition of power.

Therefore, I believe this perspective is crucial for interpreting the Isaiah passage— the mention of the new heavens and new earth in the

66th chapter signifies yet another new order, ushered in this time by our Messiah. Chapters 40-66 in the book of Isaiah constitute a message to Israel regarding the impending Messiah and a shift in the administration of God's Kingdom on earth. With this good news, the era elapsed where entry into the Kingdom was contingent upon the impossible task of adhering to His law. God ushered in the age of Grace, and gratefully, He extended it to all nations—to all people. This marks the advent of the new heavens and new earth. Interpreting Isaiah chapter 66 as foreseeing the future destruction of the world and its physical replacement is incongruent with the prophet's intended meaning and would not have been understood by his original audience.

My friend, Mike Owens, has established a website called TheHellVerses.com, where he has compiled the comments of 35 pastors, seminarians, authors, and laypersons regarding these verses and many others. Concerning the Isaiah 66 passage, Mike summarized their perspectives as follows:

> "How troubling would it be if our future home in paradise became a place where we continually observe the dead bodies of sinners, many of them our loved ones, burning, with worms persistently consuming their deceased flesh? This unsightly and disturbing scene would bring great sorrow and tears to all but the calloused."

Certainly, those who adhere to this literal interpretation presumably do not believe that worms inherit immortality. Moreover, the notion of an actual fire that never consumes the material it engulfs seems illogical in a literal sense. Continuing, the contributors on Mike's webpage believe that one is on solid ground when interpreting the 66th chapter of Isaiah as a prophetic word about a coming Messiah, portraying the suffering Savior and His return as a conquering King. This interpretation aligns with the belief that He completely dismantled the old order in 70 A.D., opening the door to a new Kingdom that would encompass all nations.

The depiction of the dead bodies of rebellious Israelites serves as imagery for the fate of mankind under the old Covenant of the Law, resulting in abhorrence, shame, and death. However, in His mercy for all,

God established a new way for everyone to enter His kingdom through the sacrifice of His Son, Jesus.

One of the contributors on Mike's page also shared this thought-provoking comment: "Figuratively, we can approach this passage with this understanding: If ALL flesh goes out and looks on the corpses of those who have 'rebelled,' whose corpses are they looking at? It would have to include at least some of them, if not all of them."

Have you ever rebelled against God? Unfortunately, some of my past actions reflect a rebellious attitude, and I look back on it with abhorrence and shame. The word "basar" is translated as "flesh." In the Septuagint, "sarc" translates the word "basar," and it is what Paul referred to as the old nature or self – as if to say, we are seeing our old rebellious selves from a resurrected state, or at least, a new enlightened perspective, just as Paul did when looking back at the former Saul. This is a portrayal of God's judgment, but there is more.

In the final part of this chapter, let us look closer at the phrase, "their worm," from the Isaiah 66 passage. What follows is my summary of an article by Alpha Omega Institute titled "Kid's Think & Believe Too!" It commences with a commentary on Psalm 22, often referred to as the Psalm of the Cross, serving as a prophetic reference to the death of Christ a thousand years before its occurrence.

In Verse 6 of this passage, it is stated: "But I am a worm, and no man" (KJV). The writer highlights that the typical Hebrew word for worm is "rimmah," signifying a maggot. However, the word Jesus uses to describe Himself in this passage is TOLA'ATH, which means "crimson worm" or "scarlet worm," with both colors being associated with blood. The crimson worm is common to the region of old Israel.

What many find intriguing about this worm is that "when it is time for the female to have babies (which she does only one time in her life), she finds the trunk of a tree, a wooden fencepost, or a stick. She then attaches her body to that wood and makes a hard, crimson shell. She is so strongly and permanently stuck to the wood that the shell can never be removed without tearing her body completely apart and killing her."

Furthermore, we learn that the mother "lays her eggs under her body and the protective shell. When the baby worms (or larvae) hatch, they stay under the shell. Not only does the mother's body give protection for her babies, but it also provides them with food – the babies feed on the LIVING body of the mother!"

When the young worms grow to the point that they can take care of themselves, usually within a few days, the mother dies. At that moment "she oozes a crimson or scarlet red dye which not only stains the wood she is attached to, but also her young children. They are colored scarlet red for the rest of their lives."

And after **three days**, the dead mother's body loses its color and turns into a white wax, like snow, which falls to the ground. The writer closes his publication with this scripture: "Come now, and let us reason together, saith the LORD: though your sins be as scarlet, they shall be as white as snow; though they be red like crimson, they shall be as wool" Isaiah 1:18, (KJV).

This is one of the most beautiful articles I have ever read, especially when I grasped that Jesus was their worm—the worm of those who had rejected Him and hung Him on a tree, His enemies. The only distinction between their worm and the crimson worm is that while the mother dies initially, so that her offspring can live, Jesus resurrects and does not remain dead. Paired with the comprehension that "their fire" here is His jealous love for Israel, which cannot be "quenched," we encounter a beautiful depiction of the depth of God's love—one that never gives up and will not fail.

This is why Paul could write the following in Romans 11:25-33:

> "I do not want you to be ignorant of this mystery, brothers (Gentiles), so that you may not be conceited: Israel has experienced a hardening in part until the full number of the Gentiles has come in. 26. **And so all Israel will be saved**, as it is written: 'The deliverer will come from Zion; He will turn godlessness away from Jacob. 27. And this is my covenant with them **when I take away (remove) their sins.'** 28. As far as the gospel is concerned, **they are enemies** on your account; but as far as election is concerned, **they are loved** on account of the patriarchs, 29. For God's gifts (faith, hope, and love) and **His call are irrevocable. 30.** Just as you who were at one time disobedient to God have now received mercy as a result of their disobedience, 31. so they too may now receive mercy as a result of God's mercy

to you. 32. For (or because) **God has bound all men over to disobedience so that He may have mercy on them all.** 33. Oh, the depth of the riches of the wisdom and knowledge of God! How unsearchable are His judgments, and His paths beyond tracing out" (NIV).

There it is again! In verse 26 God promises to take away/remove Israel's sins, just as He did with Paul, after spending three days in darkness. That is His decision, His judgment, and it sounds to me like the process when He places the grapes "in the winepress of His wrath." (We will discuss this in more detail later in the book.)

To further illustrate the passion, power, and breadth of His love, I now want to direct your attention to Ezekiel 5:5-11. In this passage, God declares that Israel had become more unruly than all the other nations around them and had not even adhered to the standards of those neighboring nations! Subsequently, in chapter 16, God asserts that Israel was worse than Sodom and Samaria. However, due to His unwavering love for them, in that same chapter, God promises to restore the fortunes of all three!

This same kind of restoration is pledged for Egypt, Assyria, and Israel in Isaiah chapter 19:19-25. The concluding verse of that chapter reads: "The Lord Almighty will bless them, saying, 'Blessed be Egypt my people, Assyria my handiwork, and Israel my inheritance'" (NIV).

What I find intriguing is how Israel, despite ultimately being saved and restored, ranks third in both comparative cases just mentioned. God views their former sinful condition as worse than that of the other nations around them. It is also noteworthy how the other two nations within each group of three are also restored. Neither Sodom nor Samaria in the first comparison, nor Egypt nor Assyria in the second, were deserving of God's grace. That is why it is called unmerited favor.

Romans 15:9 provides us with the outcome of His love for all: "so that the Gentiles may glorify God for his mercy" (NIV), particularly when they come to the realization of the words previously cited in Romans 11:32: "For God has bound all men over to disobedience so that he may have mercy on them all" (NIV).

Our God is so good; there is no limit to His love and mercy.

6

The Lake of Fire

ONE MAY WONDER how all in Israel could be saved if only a remnant accepted Jesus as their Messiah. Does this imply that most will be cast into the lake of fire, where there is no escape? Alternatively, is this prophecy about some future date when all of Israel at that time will become believers? If so, how fortunate would it be to be born in that generation, as opposed to all others.

Furthermore, if that last idea is true, we should inquire: "What did it take to get that generation to believe? What circumstances were created to prompt all of Israel to accept their Messiah at the end? And if God knows how to do it, then why didn't He create the same conditions for all other generations who needed His mercy just as desperately as any other?" That does not seem fair.

Perhaps the answer is that God does know exactly what to do, and due to His fairness and unwavering love for them, He will create the environment and circumstances necessary for His former enemies to repent and accept Him as their Messiah. Maybe the lake of fire is precisely what they need. Perhaps this is where they will be purified by the unquenchable fire of His love for them—a love that never gives up and will not fail.

The way it is translated, Revelation 20:15 informs us that those whose names are not written in the Book of Life are "cast" or "thrown" into the lake of fire. However, please read Strong's definition of the word translated as "cast" or "thrown." Strong's 906: (a) I cast, throw, rush, (b) **often** (emphasis mine), in the weaker sense: I place, put, drop.

There are multiple examples of it being used in a "weaker sense," as in Mark 7:30 when the girl was found "laid upon the bed" after Jesus had cast out the unclean spirit, and in Luke 7:20 where a beggar named Lazarus was placed at the rich man's gate. Furthermore, does it sound like Jesus to grab the back of His enemy's shirt with one hand and the seat of the man's pants with the other, as He throws them into a lake of fire?

John 5:22 informs us that the Father will not judge us, but He gives that responsibility to His Son—the One who said He came not to judge the world but to save it. Does the image of Jesus throwing people into fire represent a good portrayal of who He really is and what He came to do?

Perhaps Jesus places, puts, or lays them in the lake for their benefit – for their purification. Maybe their immersion symbolizes death to their old self, and their resurrection out of that same lake is symbolic of their new life in Christ. That sounds to me like a baptism by fire.

I believe that Romans 6:4-8 symbolically references His plan for His former enemies in the second death, the lake of fire. This is how all Israel shall be saved:

> "4. We were therefore buried with him through baptism into death in order that, just as Christ was raised from the dead through the glory of the Father, we too may live a new life. 5. For if we have been united with him in a death like his, we will certainly also be united with him in a resurrection like his. 6. For we know that our old self was crucified with him so that the body ruled by sin might be done away with, that we should no longer be slaves to sin 7. because anyone who has died has been set free from sin. 8. Now if we died with Christ, we believe that we will also live with him" (NIV).

Furthermore, in the 21st chapter of Revelation, John describes the great city, the holy Jerusalem, as "descending out of heaven from God." In verse 3 of the 22nd chapter, we find there is no evil inside the city. And in verse 15 of that final chapter, we find that "those outside the city are those who have strayed away from God, and the sorcerers and immoral and murderers and idolaters, and all who love to lie, and do so" (Living Bible). This is a description of people in outer darkness—the lake of fire.

But notice, the gates to the New Jerusalem are always open (Revelation 21:25). "Its gates never close" (Living Bible). And there are three entrances on each side of the city for a total of twelve open gates! The following comes from my friend, George Sarris, in his booklet: How Wide Are Heaven's Doors? On pages 43 and 44, George writes:

> At the very end of the last book of the Bible, we learn of a glorious city that has come down from heaven, filled with beauty that is beyond description. We are told the gates of the city are always open. The fruit of the tree of life is always available. Its leaves are for the healing of the nations. And at that time, there will no longer be any curse. Then, Jesus Himself says, "Blessed are those who wash their robes, that they may have the right to the tree of life and **may go through the gates into the city.**" (Emphasis is mine from the NIV – Revelation 22:14).

> So, who are those outside the city who are invited to wash their robes and go through the gates into the city? They're the same ones who, just a few verses earlier, were said to have their place in the Lake of Fire. Like the Prodigal Son, they are living outside the blessings of their Father. Why? Because those who are ungodly and impure are not allowed to enter through any of the city's twelve gates—while they remain in that state.

> But God does not give up on them. In the New Jerusalem, an invitation is given, "The Spirit and the bride say, 'Come.' And let him who hears say, 'Come.' Let the one who is thirsty come, and let the one who wishes take the free gift of the water of life" (Revelation 22:17, NIV).

> The bride is the body of believers throughout history who are already in the New Jerusalem. They do not need to wash their robes and eat of the tree of life because they have already done so. They are already in the city. The Spirit and

the bride are calling those in the Lake of Purifying Fire outside the gates.

Wonderfully said George! Thank you for letting me share it in this manuscript. And may I add the obvious, the gates will not remain open so those dwelling in the city may leave to live a life in outer darkness. Rather, as George stated, the gates are open as an invitation to those who desire to come out of the darkness.

Remember the Angel who came out from the altar announcing the third harvest? He had power over fire. I believe that messenger is Jesus—the One who holds the keys to death and Hades (Revelation 1:18). I believe He is the One doing the baptizing.

This leads us to the next question—Exactly what is the lake of fire and brimstone? First, here are a few scriptures "on fire," so to speak.

- We know that God is a consuming fire (Hebrews 12:29).
- Everyone will be salted with it (Mark 9:49).
- We are tested with fire to bring us to rich fulfillment (Psalms 66:10-12).
- God will baptize us, all flesh (Joel 2:28), with the Holy Spirit and with fire (Matthew 3:11).
- He came to cast fire on the earth (Luke 12:47-49).
- We are tested by fire and saved through it (1 Corinthians 3:15).

In summary, God's unquenching fire consumes, preserves (that is the meaning behind "salted"), refines, purifies, and purges us for our benefit. Remember how the barley and the wheat were both cooked in fire and made into bread?

Furthermore, the literal "fire" described as "unquenchable" in the Old Testament, and referred to by Jesus, no longer burns - Jeremiah 17:4, 27. However, it could not be quenched UNTIL it had accomplished its mission.

Now, I will summarize a story told by Dr. Kim West. It is about a group of women who were studying the book of Malachi. During the study, they read a scripture which says: "He will sit as a refiner and purifier of silver." Evidently, this verse caught their attention, and one of the ladies volunteered to find out more about the process of refining silver and report back to the group at their next Bible study. This very wise woman called a silversmith and made an appointment to watch him as he performed the refining process.

As she watched, he explained during the refining, "one needed to hold the silver in the middle of the fire where the flames were hottest as to burn away all the impurities." The woman thought some more about that verse, and she asked the silversmith "if it was true that he had to sit there in front of the fire the whole time the silver was being refined." The silversmith answered in the affirmative and added, "he not only had to sit there holding the silver, but he had to keep his eyes on the silver the entire time it was in the fire. If the silver was left even a moment too long in the flames, it would be damaged."

Then, the woman asked, "How do you know when the silver is fully refined?" He replied, "Oh, that's easy. When I see my image in it."

Dr. Kim ends the story with these encouraging words: "If today you are feeling the heat of this world's fire, just remember that God the Father and His Son Jesus Christ are refining you. You are predestined to be conformed to the image of Christ."

What a great story! Thank you for sharing it, Dr. Kim.

Next, one of my dear friends in Christ is Dr. Boyd Purcell. He wrote the following and gave me permission to share it in this book:

> "The Holy Bible is one of the most highly symbolic/ metaphorical books in the world! Excellent examples: mountains singing/skipping like rams; hills singing/ skipping like lambs; trees and floods clapping their hands (Ps. 98:8; 114:4-6; Isa.55:12). Jesus' followers: the salt of the earth and light of the world (Mt. 5:13-14). Disciples: wise as serpents and harmless as doves (Mt. 10:16). False prophets: wolves (Mt. 7:15). Legalists: strain out a gnat but swallow a camel (Mt. 23:24). Riches: easier for a camel to go through the eye of a needle than for rich people to enter the kingdom of heaven (Mt. 19:24; Mk. 10:25; Lu. 18:25). Pharisees: whitewashed tombs (Mt. 23:27-29). Hypocrites: serpents/vipers (Mt. 23:33). Speech: seasoned with salt (Col. 4:6). Many things Jesus taught in parables [often using hyperbole] (Mt. 13:3,10; Mk. 4:2,11,33). Jesus: hen/bread/

wine/blood/word/light/lamb/water/door/shepherd/way/
truth/life/vine/alpha/omega/sun (Mt.23:37; 26:26-28;
John 1:1-14, 29; 4:10-14; 10:7-14; 14:6; 15:1; Rev. 1:11-16).
In regard to fire in The Holy Bible . . . **the fire symbolizes
purification** as surely as the sky is blue and grass is green!"
(Emphasis mine.)

Boyd adds: "There is also symbolic meaning in the Greek word for fire,
the letters for "Pi Upsilon Rho," are transliterated into English as, "pur," (see
Strong's 4442) from which, via Latin, we get our English words: pure, purify,
purity, purification, purge, and purgatory. Therefore, purification is implicit
in the Greek word for fire, even if not explicitly stated."

Boyd also points out that: "Various cultures use their
particular word for "fire" in a variety of ways. In English,
we have well-known everyday expressions that are well-
understood by people all across our societal and social
spectrum. For example, if a sports commentator said that
a particular coach was the very best at getting his team
fired up for the big game, would anyone believe that coach
literally set his players on fire? If a politician were to
announce that she is not going to run for reelection, because
she no longer has the fire in her belly, would anyone, with
common sense, believe that she literally had had fire in
her abdomen? If a worker said that he went into work as
usual, and, unexpectedly, his boss called him into her office
and fired him, would anyone believe this worker had been
literally set on fire by his employer? Biblical writers used
fire in the same figurative/symbolic ways."

Thank you, Boyd, for providing additional insights on this subject.

Now, let us explore some thoughts from a few early Church Fathers.
We'll begin with Clement of Alexandria (150-213 AD): "Fire is conceived as
a benefit and strong power, destroying what is base, preserving what is good;
therefore, this fire is called 'wise' by the prophets." He further described this
fire as "saving and disciplinary, leading to conversion."

Ralph Neighbour, a Baptist minister, referred to Clement and our next Church Father, Origen, as the first "university men." St. Clement taught at the Catechetical School in Alexandria and was highly regarded as a theologian with expertise in philosophy and Greek literature. It has been said that he was surpassed only by one of his students, Origen, who is often described as having the greatest mind among the Church Fathers.

Origen (185-254 AD) expressed, "As, therefore, we say God is a consuming fire, what is it that is to be consumed by Him? We say it is wickedness, and whatever proceeds from it, figuratively called 'wood, hay, and stubble,' which denote the evil works of man. Our God is a consuming fire in this sense; and He shall come as a refiner's fire to purify rational nature from the alloy of wickedness and other impure matter that has adulterated the intellectual gold and silver; consuming whatever evil is mixed in all the soul."

Bishop Titus of Bostra (?-378 AD) emphasized, "The punishments of God are holy, as they are remedial and salutary in their effect upon transgressors; for they are inflicted, not to preserve their wickedness, but to make them cease from their sins. The abyss... is indeed the place of punishment, but... the anguish of their sufferings compels them to break off from their sins."

Since the lake of fire not only destroys evil, but also produces the opposite, the antithesis of whatever is put into it, many see it as symbolic of the presence of God. As with the face of Moses, and as with Saul's heart and mind, things change in His presence.

For example, death is placed into the lake and is destroyed. And how do you destroy death? The answer: By giving life.

Hades (the grave) is consigned to it. Hades is a place of darkness, the abode of the buried, and the realm of the unseen and the unknown. If these elements are destroyed, what is the opposite outcome? What eliminates these aspects? The answers in sequence: light, things that are uncovered (resurrected), things that are seen, and things that are known.

Unbelievers, enemies of God, and those whose names are not in the Book of Life are also cast into it. How are each of these eradicated? The answer: by replacing unbelief with belief, by transforming enemies into friends, and by conferring new names which are in the Book of Life, just as happened with Saul/Paul.

The beast is also put into it. It is the beast within each one of us that believes we can attain tranquility and happiness with enough money (Babylon), with enough power (Medes and Persians), with enough wisdom and knowledge (Greece), and with enough control through law (Romans). That beast within will be destroyed by the Spirit of Love living in our hearts.

Lastly, the false prophet is cast into it. The false prophet, who whispered in our minds from the beginning that man is self-sufficient and in control, continues his deception to this day by asserting that people are justified by their actions and decisions under the law. This form of self-righteousness is dismantled by the power of truth in His presence as we are justified (fixed) by the faith of Jesus through His work on the Cross alone. Without His faith and His work, there would be no resurrection of the dead.

As for brimstone, it is sulfur, and the Greek word for it is theion. Its root is "theo," which is translated as God. Sulfur has an atomic number of 16, a number in the Bible symbolic of never-ending love. Moreover, sulfur was considered sacred to the ancient Greeks and used in religious ceremonies to cleanse and purify their temples. They also applied it to their bodies as a symbol of consecration to God. "Theou" means to "make divine or dedicate to God."

Also, according to an article on Georgia Gulf Sulfur Corporation's website, sulfur is the workhorse of chemistry. Throughout history, sulfur/brimstone has been used to elevate the world's standard of living. It is a recognized cleansing agent, purifier, preservative, and a form of it is used in fertilizers to enhance food production.

Another consideration should be given to the word "hell." The original English term meant "to put in the ground." However, many believe that "hell" refers to the lake of fire—a place of eternal conscious torment with no escape. First, let us explore a few common-sense questions from a former Christian friend, Gary Amirault, who passed away in 2021. While he was alive, Gary posed some questions and wrote some comments on the subject, and below is a brief summary of them:

> "Hell cannot be the lake of fire, because hell is thrown into the lake and is destroyed, just like death is destroyed. So, what the hell is hell?

Here are some facts from God's Word – Thirty-one references to hell in the O.T. KJV are all translations of sheol, meaning "the grave." Those have been corrected in most modern translations. In the KJV, of the twenty-four times hell is mentioned in the N.T., ten come from the translation of hades, which is the Greek equivalent for sheol, the grave, thirteen come from gehenna, a reference to the garbage dump outside of Jerusalem, and one from tartaros, a holding place for fallen angels.

So, if it referred to a place of eternal torment, why didn't the Apostle Paul, who was commissioned to preach to the nations, warn anyone of it in any of his letters? Better yet, why didn't he warn them repeatedly? Didn't Paul say in Acts 20:27 he had declared the entire counsel of God?

Why isn't it mentioned even once in the book of Acts in any of the evangelistic sermons that were recorded by the early apostles? As a matter of fact, hell as a translation of hades or gehenna does not appear in any of the Epistles! Paul never used gehenna, and his only reference to hades was in celebration of its defeat! Only 2 Peter 2:4 mentions a place called tartaros" as a temporary holding place for fallen angels."

Thank you, Gary, for leaving us with more to consider on this topic. See you soon!

Another insightful question to ponder is: Does Matthew 25 teach that we will be sent to hell for not feeding the hungry or visiting the sick? Surprisingly, there is not a single mention in this entire passage that "belief in Jesus" is the distinguishing factor between the sheep and the goats. Perhaps our Lord's words were specifically directed at His audience at that time; maybe they were aimed at the Scribes and Pharisees. (We will explore this parable in a little more depth later in the book.) For further information on the points raised about hell, if possible, please watch the profoundly moving YouTube video titled "Hallelujah in Hell." It is truly awe-inspiring.

All the information above has been presented for your contemplation. It may not align with what you have heard in the past on these topics, but it is not new. This theme reflects the beliefs of many of the Greek-speaking early Church Fathers.

Next, we will explore another topic that might, at first glance, seem to be an obstacle to God's forgiveness of His former enemies – the unpardonable sin. I feel the need to cover this topic out of respect for those who may not have previously considered the idea that people can be resurrected from the lake of fire.

7

The Unpardonable Sin

MATTHEW 12:31-32 (KJV) states, "All manner of sin and blasphemy shall be forgiven unto men; but blasphemy against the Holy Ghost shall not be forgiven unto men. And whoever speaks a word against the Son of Man, it shall be forgiven him, but whoever speaks against the Holy Spirit, it shall not be forgiven him, neither in this world nor in the world to come."

Similarly, in Mark 3:28-29 (KJV), Jesus declares, "Verily I say unto you, all sins shall be forgiven unto the sons of men, and blasphemies wherewith soever they shall blaspheme: But he that shall blaspheme against the Holy Ghost hath never forgiveness, but is in danger of eternal damnation."

These passages convey a stern message, indicating that blasphemy against the Holy Ghost is an unpardonable sin. Despite the explicit language, there are differing interpretations of it. Some argue that faith in the atoning work of Jesus results in the forgiveness of all sins—past, present, and future. According to this perspective, confessing sins fosters intimate fellowship with God, but unrepentant sins do not impact a believer's eternal destiny, as it is determined at the moment of receiving Christ.

So, what is the answer? Well, there is much to explore here, and I hope to articulate my understanding with respect to those who may have a different one.

Let us initiate our discussion by examining the backdrop of the story in Matthew and Mark. At that moment, Jesus had just performed a miraculous healing on a man who was both deaf and blind. In the cultural context of the Middle East during that time, such physical conditions were often associated with demon possession. But regardless of whether the man was actually possessed, the focus should have been on celebrating the extraordinary restoration of sight and hearing.

If we had been present, some of us might have joyfully exclaimed in our best Austin Powers style, "Yeah, baby," followed by a triumphant fist pump, akin to Tiger Woods' "Yes!" However, the Scribes and Pharisees present did not share in the celebration. Instead, they accused Jesus of expelling the devil by the prince of devils.

It is hard to comprehend how a group of people could twist such a remarkable miracle into something so malevolent. These self-proclaimed experts in holiness were so out of sync with God that they could not discern good from evil, even when it was right in front of them. Jesus decisively refuted them, skillfully turning their own beliefs against them, a feat underscored with a bit of historical context.

William Barclay, in his commentary on Matthew, explains that, according to Jewish teaching, the Holy Spirit served two primary functions. First, it conveyed truth to individuals, and second, it aided them in recognizing and understanding that truth. In simpler terms, it assisted in discerning between right and wrong, good and evil. Jesus skillfully utilized this understanding against them.

In verse 35, Jesus declares, "A good man out of the good treasure of the heart bringeth forth good things: an evil man out of the evil treasure bringeth forth evil things" (KJV). He also challenges them by saying in verse 33: "Either make the tree good, and his fruit good; or else make the tree corrupt, and his fruit corrupt; for the tree is known by his fruit" (KJV).

Essentially, Jesus conveys two crucial points: what he did was good, and what they said was evil. He emphasizes that their inability to distinguish between good and evil implies the absence of the Holy Spirit within them. This revelation undoubtedly struck a chord with them.

Moreover, Jesus offers three straightforward explanations for why, if he cast out a demon, it was only because he was opposing Satan. With each assertion, Jesus firmly put the Scribes and Pharisees in their place. According to Barclay and other scholars, this confrontation marked a turning point, as the religious leaders begin plotting to kill him.

Barclay highlights an essential observation, noting that when Rabbis began a parable, they often introduced it with, "There was a son of man who..." equivalent to our saying, "There was a man." Barclay explains that this phrase was used in the Old Testament to refer to a man, as seen when God addresses Ezekiel: "Son of man, stand on your feet..." In this context, Barclay suggests that Jesus might have meant the Pharisees could be forgiven for showing contempt toward another man, just like any other sin. However, the King James Version states that there will be no forgiveness "in this world, neither in the world to come" for blasphemy against the Holy Spirit. Notably, the Greek word used here is "aion," not "kosmos," prompting most translations to correct "world" to "age."

Clearly, Jesus possessed insight into the hearts of the Scribes and Pharisees, as well as foresight into their future. He understood that they would not repent during the era they were currently living in, operating under the covenant of the law. Furthermore, He knew that they would persist in their unchanged behavior throughout their lifetime in the next age, governed by the covenant of grace. Jesus anticipated that these Pharisees would witness both ages unfold before their passing from this life, yet He also foresaw that they would remain unswayed from their malevolent ways during that entire period.

We can only envision the gravity in our Lord's voice as He uttered those piercing words about forgiveness, locking eyes with these religious leaders. Consequently, scholars like Barclay interpret our Lord's statements about forgiveness as a prophetic warning specifically aimed at those leaders.

Regrettably, the reality unfolded as anticipated – there was no change in their behavior, nor did the nation of Israel alter its course. They not only continued to slander Jesus, but escalated it to the point of orchestrating His crucifixion. Subsequently, they extended their blasphemy to those filled with the Holy Spirit, commissioned to spread the Good News to the nations. This relentless opposition is the epitome of blasphemy. The consequence was severe, with Israel facing destruction at the hands of the Romans in 70 A.D.

For those who remain unconvinced by Barclay's arguments and still believe that our Lord's warning about blasphemy applies universally, with no forgiveness for those who commit such an act, consider 1 Timothy 1:13. In this passage, Paul unequivocally admits to having been guilty of "blasphemy." Yet, remarkably, he declares that he has been forgiven.

Did Paul blaspheme against the work of the Holy Spirit? Indeed, his actions were incredibly slanderous, irreverent, and insulting. He actively opposed, threatened, arrested, convicted, and participated in the murder of those who were filled with the Spirit and guided by it. However, when confronted with his sin and comprehended the forgiveness extended to him through Jesus' sacrifice on the Cross, Paul embarked on a transformative journey. This journey granted him a profound understanding of the term "grace" – unmerited favor.

At that juncture, he became profoundly remorseful for his past actions and underwent a process of repentance. Throughout this repentance, he found himself blinded **for three days, a period marked by total darkness,** and likely accompanied by weeping, and possibly even some gnashing of teeth. Gnashing of teeth typically arises from pain, anger, or anguish. In Saul's case, it wasn't physical pain or anger that prompted this reaction. Rather, it was likely a profound sense of anguish over the hurt and harm he had inflicted. This anguish manifested itself when he abstained from food and drink during those three days.

Sent to a place of darkness and death, **the old Saul perished**, giving way to a new creature in Christ, symbolizing a resurrection—now known as Paul. In Galatians 2:20, Paul succinctly expressed this transformation: "I have been crucified with Christ, and I myself no longer live, but Christ lives in me" (Living Bible).

Given his transformation from a former adversary, Paul fervently proclaimed in Romans 8:38-39 that nothing could separate us from God's love in Christ, alluding to the "unquenchable fire" of His love, even for a former enemy. In 1 Timothy 1:16, Paul declared that he received mercy so that God could put on display His patience, "that in me first Jesus Christ might shew forth all long-suffering, **for a pattern of others** about to believe in Him" (YLT).

The picture God is drawing for us, the outline sketch, seems to involve individuals in God's household following a trajectory akin to Saul's— engaging in various sins, and subsequently experiencing a revelation of Jesus' atoning work. This journey is accompanied by a season of shame (darkness) marked by acknowledgment of sins with weeping and anguish over the harm caused.

Does this path also encompass a death to self and the resurrection of a new creature wherein Christ permanently resides? Did Christ, through the act of crucifixion, take away Saul's sins? The picture emerging from

THE UNPARDONABLE SIN

this narrative indeed suggests that this is the transformative journey God is illustrating in the outline.

Nonetheless, there are still some lingering issues in this passage from Mark concerning the concept of the "unpardonable sin" that require further review before a conclusion can be reached. For example, the term "never" in the expression "hath never forgiveness," as seen in some translations of Mark 3:29, is, in fact, derived from the Greek word meaning "no" or "not." Therefore, asserting an absolute "never," is an absolute error, especially when considering Paul's experience of forgiveness as evidence to the contrary.

Moreover, as previously discussed, the translation of "aionios" as "eternal" is disputable. Paul's forgiveness serves as additional evidence supporting the better translation of this adjective as "age-lasting." Additionally, the previously examined, man-made term, "damnation," does not make any sense either, given the above.

Dr. Daniel Wallace sheds light on the construction of the phrase "blaspheme against the Holy Ghost hath never forgiveness." The verb is in the present tense, indicative mood, and active voice. These grammatical elements emphasize the subject rather than time, aligning more with a present condition, than predicting the future. It shares similarities with the aorist tense, offering a snapshot of an event, without any reference to permanency.

Hence, those Jesus addressed at that time—the Scribes, Pharisees, and Israel as a nation—were the focal point. Due to their rejection of the Savior, they would not ask for forgiveness of their sins in their current state. Consequently, they remained unaltered in their behavior and refrained from repentance in that existing condition.

In contrast, Saul, a former Pharisee, later comprehended the atoning work of Christ on the Cross, even for blasphemy committed out of ignorance. His judgment for these transgressions, and many others, took the form of forgiveness—an undeserved favor—from the One who preemptively removed, or took away his sins even before their commission.

In summary, the threat of damnation for one who blasphemes, if one were to entertain that perspective, was not eternal. Furthermore, the notion of "never" being forgiven, proved to be inaccurate as well. I cannot come to a different conclusion.

I liken Jesus' words in Mark to a parental figure issuing a stern warning to their children: "If you do ____ (fill in the blank), you will be put in time out, and under no circumstances will I let you off the hook! DO YOU UNDERSTAND ME?" (In my childhood neighborhood, parents often promised to use the belt; "time outs" were reserved for sports.) Sometimes, out of deep love for our children, we need to be loud and stern to prevent them from causing harm to themselves or others. In such instances, shouting "I'll never forgive you!" would be entirely out of place.

As previously noted, Jesus foresaw that Israel would endure an extended period of darkness after the destruction of their nation by the Romans in 70 A.D. However, scripture indicates that God's work with them is not concluded. As mentioned earlier, "all Israel shall be saved." The unquenchable fire of God's love for them will persist, accomplishing its mission—removing their sins and fostering repentance and a change in behavior.

Jesus illustrated this sentiment in the 15th chapter of Luke, verses 4-7: "What man of you, having a hundred sheep, if he has lost one of them, does not leave the ninety-nine in the wilderness, and go after the one which is lost, until He finds it? And when he has found it, he lays it on His shoulders, rejoicing. And when he comes home, he calls his friends and his neighbors, saying to them, 'Rejoice with me, for I have found my sheep which was lost.' Just so, I tell you, there will be more joy in heaven over one sinner who repents than over ninety-nine righteous persons who need no repentance" (RSV).

In this, we witness Jesus taking complete responsibility for His lost sheep, symbolically bearing them on His shoulders, much like He did with the Cross of Calvary. This parable conveys the one lost sheep represents a sinner who has strayed. The uplifting news is that Jesus actively pursues this lost soul until He finds it and safely brings it back into the fold. He rescues it from perishing because the Lord is unwaveringly committed to saving each one—His passion emanates from His unquenchable love. As a result, He doesn't settle for 99% but reclaims 100% of His sheep.

Moreover, the laws of redemption outlined in the 25th chapter of Leviticus prescribe that the nearest kinsman must return and redeem what his relative has lost. If the redeemer possessed the capability to redeem, the law mandates him, by the Will of our Father in heaven, to restore what his brother had lost.

Additionally, in the case of a bondservant indebted to a master, the master could not retain the individual in servitude if the near kinsman paid the debt. The near kinsman held the right of redemption to set the bondservant free, even if the bondservant resisted. The authority to decide rested with the near kinsman, and he had the final say in the matter.

Jesus, born as a Jew and in the likeness of men, stood as Israel's near kinsman, paying all their debts on the Cross. Possessing His Father's direction, authority, and means, He had the capacity to redeem all His sheep, even if they momentarily strayed or resisted redemption. Above all, He had the heart, will, and passion to undertake such a profound act of love.

Jeremiah 9:24 further emphasizes this compassionate nature of God: "I am the Lord who exercises kindness, justice, and righteousness on earth, for in these things I delight" (NIV). The Living Bible interprets the concluding phrase as: "I love to be this way." God takes pleasure in showing kindness, rectifying situations, making things right, and is exceedingly capable of doing it.

Hence, in my perspective, there is no such concept as an unpardonable sin. When sinners comprehend the extent of what God accomplished for them on the Cross, they are moved to shame and prompted to alter their behavior, even if they were once adversaries, similar to Saul.

These recent chapters are intended to open a door in your mind to the possibility that God may rescue His enemies from the lake of fire in a third resurrection. While I acknowledge that I may not have addressed all your questions, my hope is that the light filtering through this partially opened door will kindle your curiosity enough to encourage further reading.

Now we arrive at the most thrilling segment of the book, at least from my perspective. I have previously introduced a few examples of the recurring pattern of "threes." All of them point to the three distinct groups slated for resurrection. In the upcoming chapter, we will uncover several more instances where this pattern exists. We will explore their implications in more detail, and I believe you will find it to be fascinating.

8

Patterns

TOWARDS THE END of Chapter 3, after highlighting the significance of the barley, wheat, and grape harvests, I made the assertion that God's communion with mankind is not complete until the bread and the wine are made ready and served. Now you know the direction I am heading.

The phrase, "while they were eating," has prompted various theories about the menu at the Last Supper. According to Jewish traditions, the Passover meal could have featured a range of dishes, including beans, a green salad, olives, dates, honeycomb, fish, and possibly lamb. Articles from

"Christianity Today," "Smithsonian Magazine," and other online sources from diverse scholars, confirm these dishes as plausible options based on the traditions surrounding this meal.

The key point to emphasize is that, among the various items potentially consumed that night, Jesus specifically mentions the bread and wine. Could there be significance in this choice? I strongly believe the answer is a resounding "Yes!" I contend that the bread and wine symbolize the three groups slated for resurrection.

While partaking in the meal, Jesus broke the bread and then took a cup, filling it with wine. The imagery is unmistakable – two pieces of bread and a cup of wine.

Regarding the consumption of these elements, both Luke and Paul included Jesus' words: "Do this in remembrance of me" (Luke 22:19 & 1 Corinthians 11:24, NIV). Essentially, Jesus was instructing His followers to remember something about him while partaking in this act. He proclaimed Himself as the Lord of the Harvest, the One responsible for transforming barley and wheat into bread, symbolized by the breaking of that bread. He also claimed responsibility for the grape harvest and the conversion of grapes into wine.

For the past 2000 years, Jesus established a poignant reminder for us – that His body was broken and His blood was spilled, **for the removal of our iniquities.** Notice His broken body is compared to the bread that was broken. It is clear, the two pieces of bread refer to His body, and this is why the first two bread groups were known as "the Body of Christ." And His blood was poured out like wine, after the grapes were placed under His feet in the winepress of His wrath. In this, Jesus identifies with all three resurrected groups. They are all **in Him,** and that is why Paul could write: "as in Adam all die, so **in Christ** all shall be made alive," as I quoted earlier.

At the moment of His death, He declared, "It is finished" (the removal of sin). Simultaneously, the veil in the Temple that separated God and man was torn in two. The decision made by one man, Adam, led humanity down an unwanted path of death and separation from fellowship with God. Now, the choice of another man, Jesus, guides humanity back to God, resulting in life and the restoration of that fellowship.

Consider this additional aspect about Jesus. The Adversary made a desperate attempt to thwart God's plans when Jesus underwent three tests at the beginning of His ministry. In the initial test, Jesus was challenged to take stones from the wilderness and transform them into bread to satisfy His hunger—His desire. I interpret these stones as representatives of the first harvest—the harvest of barley. In this trial, Jesus was urged to take that bread and forgo the rest. Essentially, the Adversary suggested that the bread from the barley harvest would satisfy His desire. Satan was profoundly mistaken.

Jesus countered, asserting that man (all men) could not live by Him taking that bread alone. In other words, His Father's plans would not be fulfilled by taking that bread group only; additional crops would need to be harvested as well. Moreover, Jesus emphasized that humanity would live by the declarations emanating from the mouth of God—declarations encompassing the blessing of all families, nations, and peoples through His Son's sacrifice on the Cross. These declarations would not be confined to the salvation of those in the first resurrection—the barley group.

Having successfully navigated the first test, the Adversary then took Jesus to the highest point on the Temple grounds, in full view of those who worshipped God. He suggested that if Jesus were to descend (abandon His role as the Lord of the Harvests), He would be unharmed by the stones on the Temple grounds.

Drawing on 1 Peter 2:5, which describes God's people as living stones forming a spiritual house, it becomes evident that the stones on the Temple grounds would not harm our Lord's ministry, because they believed and belonged to Him. I propose that this second group of stones represents the wheat from the second harvest—those who are His at His coming. Once again, Jesus declined Satan's offer, recognizing that there is another crop to be harvested—the grapes.

This prompts a question: Have we as Christians succumbed to one or both of the first two temptations—take the bread groups and disregard the rest? In general, it certainly seems that we have. And if we have, it might fulfill our desires, but not those of our Father. He desires that last group—the wine—just as much as the bread.

Realizing that Jesus would not be content with the bread groups alone, the adversary then led Jesus to a high mountain. Why a mountain? And which mountain?

The first time I explored this passage in connection to the three resurrections, I faced a roadblock. While I could see the first two groups of stones possibly representing the initial two resurrected groups, I struggled to identify another group of stones for the third resurrection. However, the next day, I felt prompted to look up the definition of a mountain. To my surprise, I discovered that a mountain is a pile of rocks (stones), either sedimentary or metamorphic, elevated over time by a great force beneath them.

Those words leaped off the page at me – a great force beneath them, lifting the rocks upward. That's when I realized this mountain, this pile of stones, symbolized the nation of Israel. They had been elevated above all other nations for the purpose of establishing God's Kingdom on earth (Isaiah 2:1-5). On this mountain, Jesus could see "all the kingdoms of the earth," and the adversary offered them all to Him. However, Jesus, refusing to worship him, rejected the offer and proceeded to fulfill His destiny as the Lord of the harvests.

To dive deeper into the story of this mountain and those involved in the third test, let us explore the accounts found in Matthew 21 and the 11th chapter of Mark. There, Jesus curses a fruitless fig tree, and when His disciples marveled at the immediate death of the tree, Jesus shared something intriguing. He said, "if ye shall say to this mountain, be thou removed, and be thou cast into the sea; it shall be done" (Matthew 21:21 – KJV).

I had always been taught that the main point of this story is that I needed to have more faith! If I did, mountains in my life could be moved. There is some truth there, but now I see I was missing the main point. Why did the focus of the conversation shift from a dead fig tree to a mountain?

The answer lies in the fact that the fig tree and this mountain were direct references to the nation of Israel. Jesus had been sent to rescue them from the curse of the law, but they rejected Him. He then foretold their fate as they would be removed as a nation and thrown into the sea of humanity in 70 A.D. at the hands of the Romans.

Moreover, Jesus pronounced to that tree, "May you never bear fruit again" Matthew 21:19 (NIV). In perfect alignment with these words, Mark informs us that afterward, Jesus went to the Temple and cleansed it. Reading the 23rd chapter of Matthew will provide a good overview of how Jesus felt about those in His own household who rejected Him. They had become His enemies.

In the 24th and 25th chapters of Matthew, He ministered to the disciples and apprised them of the impending judgment that would befall that generation in Israel, along with the reasons for it. As three examples, He instructed His disciples to learn from the sign of the fig tree, be faithful like the wise servant, and be prepared like the five wise virgins who had oil in their lamps for the arrival of the bridegroom. (For more on the judgement that would fall on that generation in Israel, see the Appendix, where Dr. Kenneth Gentry probes the issues in detail. I believe many will find it "eye-opening," just as I did.)

Jesus also stated that there would be two different types of people in Israel. They had been called as a nation to be laborers in the field and in the mills for the harvest of the nations. The field represented the world. The individuals in Israel unprepared to accept the new covenant of Grace would be taken (removed), while those who embraced God's grace would be left behind to complete the work of the harvest. This would parallel the days of Noah when the disobedient were removed, and the righteous were left.

Those left behind to carry out that work would become a part of the stone "cut out of the mountain without human hands." We are told that this stone will crush all the kingdoms of this earth in Nebuchadnezzar's vision. It will be God's Kingdom, filling the whole earth, and it will never be destroyed; see Daniel chapter 2.

For those who rejected Him and were removed from the field and the mills, there is good news: a day is coming when "all Israel" shall be saved (Romans 11:26). This would fulfill the prophecy where many chosen to be the first to enter this Kingdom will be the last ones to do so. However, they will enter, but only after being harvested as grapes and spending some time in the winepress of His wrath, where they will be transformed into the finest wine.

I interpret the parable of the talents as depicting those in Israel who rejected Jesus as the one-talent person. They buried their talent and remained under the covenant of the law. The two-talent person, representing the wheat harvest, blends the two covenants, believing that salvation is based on the work of Jesus, plus their own actions and decisions. The five-talent person reflects the Barley crop – those who trust solely in the work of Christ alone. In the Bible, the number five represents grace.

The notion of saving those who rejected Him in this life is something traditional (not original) theology deems impossible. However, as Jesus explained to His disciples concerning the rich young ruler, even though it may seem impossible for some, like Israel, to enter the Kingdom of Heaven based on their behavior, with God, all things are possible, based on His behavior! Therefore, He promises to seek the lost sheep "until He finds it" (Luke 15:4). Taking full responsibility, He carries it on His shoulders back to safety.

His Son resisted temptations to settle for less and went to the Cross to obtain all three groups. Jesus began His ministry by passing three tests and ended it in the garden when He prayed three times: Saying, "Father, if thou be willing, remove this cup from me: nevertheless not my will, but thine, be done" (Luke 22:42, KJV). Jesus did the Father's will, and this is what He wants us to remember about Him when taking Communion.

From the beginning in Genesis, significant foreshadowing of the three groups to be resurrected can be found in the personalities of Adam's three sons: Abel, Seth, and Cain, and later in the lineage of Noah. After the flood, it has been said that all of humanity can be summed up in Noah's three boys – Shem, Ham, and Japheth.

Shem's mature personality aligns with those resurrected in the first group. He was a man of character, authority, and honor. Described as having a worldview divorced from personal gain, Shem exemplifies the qualities found in those who experience the initial resurrection. It was from his lineage that the Messiah was descended.

In contrast, Ham, the younger and less mature brother, reflected a **self-centered** nature being more concerned with personal gain, like those in the third group. Japheth's personality was the one in the middle, displaying a mixture of genuine concern for others, but also some self-centered tendencies as well. One commentator I read called him, "bi-polar."

But for me, the most notable of all these indirect references to the three groups are expressed in:

1. The fact that Jesus raised a person from the dead on three different occasions during His ministry on earth. (More on this later.)
2. Our Lord's words found in Luke 13:32: "Go tell that fox, 'I will drive out demons and heal people today and tomorrow, and on the third day I will accomplish my purpose; I will reach my goal'" (NIV). What is His purpose? He came not to judge the world, but to save it. The casting out demons is the removal of evil, and to save means to rescue or heal. With this understanding, we find Jesus sending a prophetic

message to Herod, a prince and power of this world standing in opposition to His work. He said to tell that rascal (devil) that I am going to cast evil out of men and save them today; I am going to do it a second time tomorrow, but on the third time around, I will reach my goal. In doing so, His will, will be done and accomplished.

3. And why do you suppose Jesus spent three days in the grave? Maybe this was the sign of Jonah where He would spend "three days in the earth" resurrecting people at three different times before accomplishing His purpose and reaching His goal.

I also believe it is more than coincidental that we have three manifestations of the God-Head. It appears that each one identifies with one of the three groups to be made alive.

1. The Father, who is sovereign, uses vessels in the first group to rule and reign with Him for a season.
2. The Son – His Son – who uses vessels in the second group for worship, emphasizing they are "His" at His coming.
3. The Holy Spirit, falls as fire on those to be purified in the third group. And when the Holy Spirit fills a person in this group, it engenders a natural flow of praise in words previously unutterable to them. These words were foreign to their thinking – unthinkable – like a foreign language, because when people speak in tongues, they speak words of praise directly to our Father (1 Corinthians 14:2).

Closely examining the three patriarchs of Israel – Abraham, Isaac, and Jacob – further reinforces this pattern. Abraham was the first of the faithful, the progenitor and founding father of God's chosen people. Isaac, **His** son, was the second generation, and associated with the second group who are "His at His coming." Jacob represented the third.

Jacob's name means "deceiver," as he was commonly known in the Bible for his cunning and deceitful ways, especially toward his twin brother, Esau. However, Jacob also depicts the power and grace of God to change and renew. After an all-night wrestling match with God's messenger, Jacob received a new name, just like Paul received – a name that I will bet is written in the Book of life – Israel.

In harmony with Jacob's story, the nation of Israel wrestles with their Messiah in the New Testament, as an enemy of God. They lose the match, but ultimately win because of the fire of His love for them. Let us look in more detail regarding the connection between Jacob, Israel, and those in the third group.

Dr. Bullinger commented on Jacob's wrestling match with the angel in his notes on Genesis in The Companion Bible:

> "prevailed = succeeded. He had contended for the birthright and succeeded (25:29-34). He contended for the blessing and succeeded (27). He contended with Laban and succeeded (31). He contended with 'men' and succeeded. Now he contends with God – and fails. Hence, his name was changed to Isra-el, God commands, to teach him the greatly needed lesson of dependence upon God."

To drive home the point, Dr. Bullinger adds this comment about the meaning of the name, Israel:

> "Israel = God commands, orders, rules. Man attempts it but always, in the end, fails. Out of some forty Hebrew names compounded with 'El' or 'Jah,' God is always the doer of what the verb means."

Does this sound familiar in Israel's struggle with the law? Remember how they thought that entry into the kingdom would be based upon a man's ability to fulfill the law, upon man's actions and decisions under the law? In this, they were exhibiting the character of their former predecessor, Jacob. At that stage, they wrestled with Jesus, who offered them something better, but He was unable to convince those Jacobites during his ministry on earth. However, He went to the Cross and prevailed on their behalf, so that they could be harvested in the third resurrection.

Dr. Stephen Jones from his book, The Laws of the Second Coming:

> "At Peniel Jacob learned the lesson of the sovereignty of God. He now learned that God had been behind both Esau and Laban, that God had raised up both of these men to

afflict Jacob and to teach him to stop contending... Jacob and his mother had thought that disaster was about to occur when Isaac intended to give Esau the birthright. For this reason, they plotted to give God a helping hand and take the birthright by deceit."

At Peniel, God blessed Jacob with the knowledge of His grace – that His favor would not be based upon the actions of man, but by the sovereign actions of God. With this new knowledge, His name was changed to Israel, and the following day, he could see the "face of God" even in Esau.

After this blessing, we are told that Jacob/Israel entered the Promised Land at Succoth, one of the names for the Feast of Tabernacles! There, he built a house and made booths for his livestock, all in connection with this third and final feast day celebration. It is worth repeating: After Jacob was blessed with the knowledge of God's grace, his name was changed to Israel, and he immediately entered the Promised Land at Tabernacles, just as His former enemies will do at the third resurrection.

The story of Abraham, Lot, and Sodom, in Genesis chapters 18 and 19, also provides further insights in another foreshadowing of the destinies of the three groups. This narrative also serves as a symbolic representation of Israel's future—those embracing the covenant of grace, those remaining in sin under the old covenant, and those blending the two covenants.

In Ezekiel 16:48-50 and Amos 4:1-11, God draws parallels between Sodom and Israel. In these accounts, Israel, like Sodom, mirrors Ham, Noah's son, who became lost in self-centeredness. Abraham, choosing grace, reflects Shem's character, marked by love for the Lord and concern for neighbors (nations). Lot's family exhibits traits akin to the bi-polar Japheth, and the two-talent person. His wife looks back to the old covenant, and his daughters attempt to preserve their lineage by returning to Sodom's ways.

Abraham's descendants enter the Promised Land first, while Lot's progeny, identified as Moabites and Ammonites, find themselves on the outskirts temporarily. Sodom, faces destruction, but later undergoes restoration, paralleling Israel's descendants. The promises of restoration for both groups are detailed in Ezekiel 16 and Jeremiah 49.

In God's overarching plan, all three groups eventually grasp and encounter His unmerited favor and unconditional love. This unfolds in a predetermined sequence, carefully designed, and orchestrated for the necessary training of His children as they are molded into the image of their Father. Ultimately, the three groups will be declared "holy, holy, holy."

Like Job's three daughters, who were born after his previous ones had passed away, the three groups will be renowned for their beauty. Job 42:1 highlights the exceptional beauty of them, stating, "Nowhere in all the land were there found women as beautiful as Job's daughters" (NIV). Each one possessed distinctive qualities that set them apart.

Jemimah, the first daughter, bore a name meaning "dove." The association of doves with doves with the first group is very compelling. In Matthew 10:16, Jesus sends out His chosen, those who would give their lives for Christ. Even though they would suffer tribulation, He instructed them to be as gentle and harmless as doves. The dove represents God's presence, as we saw in Matthew 3:16, when John saw the Spirit of the God descending on Jesus like a dove. These birds are small and delicate, but resilient and can survive even in inhospitable conditions, just as the first group found themselves during their lives. In Leviticus 1:14, we also find that doves were the only birds suitable for sacrifice, because in The Song of Solomon 5:12, we find they represent purity, faithfulness, and innocence, just like those in the first harvest.

The second of Job's daughters, Kezia, was named after a spice or perfume. Her connection to those in the second harvest, who are found worshipping Him at His coming, is just as profound. In the Old Testament, God commanded the priests to continually burn aromatic incense, made from a blend of five spices, with five being a symbol of His grace. As one Bible commentator wrote: "It wasn't simply the fragrance itself that pleased God, but what it represented: the constant prayers of the people." These prayers in worship are so valuable and beautiful to God that He lovingly collects them in "golden bowls" in heaven (Revelation 5:8).

The third daughter, Keren-Happuch, derived her name from an eye-shadow, and she was known for her captivating eyes. Like the darkness that overshadowed a former enemy's eyes for three days, Saul's eyes were later opened to the magnificence of His grace, and the story is beautiful! As we will discuss later in this book, this profound picture of God's grace was given to the world as an historical record for all to see what unmerited favor looks like. It is amazing how God can take the darkness over someone's eyes, and turn it into incomparable beauty! The story of Paul is captivating, and it reflects the story of those in the third harvest.

While each daughter was unique, all shared the common attribute of being "beautiful like none other." When God resurrects the three groups, they too, will be celebrated for their individual beauty, akin to Job's daughters.

Another intriguing connection can be drawn between the three groups and the narrative of the three wise men. Although the Bible does not specify the exact number of wise men, tradition suggests three due to the three distinct gifts presented to Jesus. These Magi were notable pilgrims whose gifts represented their culture, or "where they were from," as one writer stated it. Each brought gifts of adoration based on "who they were," as that same writer declared.

Gold, symbolizing royalty and reigning, was something the first group would be allowed to participate in after they were harvested. Frankincense was used as an offering to God in worship. Its pleasant aroma made it a fitting symbol of reverence. All of this aligns well with the worship practices of the second group before their harvest. Myrrh, is an embalming ointment associated with those experiencing the second death, but destined for resurrection. Ultimately, when God completes His work with each group, they all will be transformed into "WISE MEN." Each will bring their unique gift, and each will bow down and worship Him.

Perhaps additional insights into the three groups can be drawn from Sigmund Freud's personality theory, which divides the human psyche into three components: the id, ego, and superego. Saul McLeod, PHD, provides a concise summary of Freud's theories on Simple Psychology's web page. According to Freud, the id represents the primitive and instinctive aspect of personality, seeking immediate satisfaction of every wishful impulse, much like Ham. The ego serves as a mediator between the unrealistic id and the real world, akin to Japhet. It endeavors to find ways to fulfill id's demands while considering the consequences and the needs of others. On the other hand, the superego, reminiscent of Shem, functions to control the id's impulses and persuades the ego to pursue moralistic goals rather than merely satisfying the id's desires.

Another set of parallels can be drawn from Danish philosopher Soren Kierkegaard's three spheres of existence. An article by Kenny Eliason on Owlcation's web page gives us the following information about these three.

The Aesthetic Sphere, focuses on pleasure and self-indulgence, and it aligns with Ham's way of living. The Ethical Sphere introduces concepts of good, evil, and responsibility for others, reflecting the characteristics of Japhet. The Religious Sphere, is where the highest purpose is achieved through a relationship with God, and it corresponds with Shem's path.

While Freud and Kierkegaard offer insightful secular theories, numerous comparisons to the three groups can be found in other Bible passages. For instance, in II Samuel 22:2 and Psalms 18:2, David sings words that carry profound meaning for the three groups: "The Lord is my rock, my fortress, and my deliverer." Associating Peter, whose name means "rock," with those in the first group is not a stretch. And the Lord serves as the protector of those who are His at His coming, representing the second group. He is also the deliverer of those in the third group, who will experience the second death before their resurrection.

The words of Jesus in John 14:6 also emphasize His role as the Savior of the three groups, stating, "I am the way, the truth, and the life." The only way to the Father is through the Son. The people in the first group are the first to experience this reality. The second group are the ones who are found worshipping Him in spirit and in truth, and the third group may experience life after the second death.

In this chapter, I have explored fifteen passages in the Bible, plus two very well-known secular theories, with each pointing to the three groups to be resurrected. This is in addition to the three cords from John, Moses, and Paul, discussed in chapter 3. However, there are many other instances where this pattern of "three" emerges. Seven additional ones will be uncovered in the remaining chapters, and I believe that as others become aware of this pattern, they will discover many more.

These seven passages include:

1. Paul's conversion experience with three days in darkness.
2. Our Lord's first miracle—turning water into wine on the third day of the wedding feast.
3. The significance of the phrase "Holy, Holy, Holy."
4. Three groups of people found in Revelation chapter 5.
5. Paul's experience when he was caught up to the third heaven.

6. Peter's vision of three sheets of unclean animals coming down from heaven and being pronounced clean.

7. The meaning behind three groups of fourteen generations from Abraham to Christ.

For those who see, or are beginning to see the three groups to be resurrected, the next questions naturally arise: "Who participates in the third harvest? Who are these enemies?" The next chapter will provide some insights that may help answer these crucial questions.

9

The Third Group

IN THE 7TH chapter, I briefly discussed Paul's conversion experience. His former self, Saul, opposed Christ and held a prominent position among blasphemers. I consider his experience to be a foreshadowing of what individuals in the third group will undergo. His conversion initiated with a blinding light, followed by a voice from heaven, and then his judgment. This sequence mirrors the pattern of the enemies destined for the lake of fire and raised in the third group.

At the coming of our Lord, they will hear the voice of God and face judgment. Nevertheless, the previously mentioned "pattern" extends beyond this point, encompassing repentance, forgiveness, and restoration. Saul's three days as an enemy in the fire were far from pleasant. A Bible commentator aptly expressed it: "Saul was thinking, 'I'm a dead man.'" The thoughts that raced through his mind after Jesus revealed Himself as the voice behind the light, can only be imagined.

Following this revelation, he abstained from eating or drinking for three days, consumed by anguish and weeping, as he grappled with the realization of his grievous errors and the pain he had inflicted on others. I do not believe it is a coincidence that Saul endured three days with darkness over his eyes (eyeshadow) before his healing and restoration into a new life. I see this as another indicator of how this group would need to wait their turn for harvest.

While Saul possessed a limited free will, God had foreordained a plan from the beginning of time, affording him an opportunity to reconsider his misguided beliefs. This plan unfolded in a meticulously arranged three-day sequence offering insight into what might await those in the third and final harvest.

Let us explore a few more details within this pattern, this outline sketch. Saul was journeying toward "Damascus," a word that means "silent is the sackcloth weaver." The sackcloth weaver crafted garments meant for penitence, to be worn humbly as a symbol of remorse for misdeeds and improper behavior.

Saul was in route to a Gentile capital to apprehend believers, but the Silent Sackcloth Weaver was waiting for him, intending to recommission him with a completely opposing objective. This transformation exemplifies the impact of the lake of fire. Saul, whose name meant "one who asks or inquires of God," would soon be seeking sackcloth in humility once exposed to the truth.

The lake of fire serves as a realm of humility and repentance. Saul was led meekly by the hand to the house of Judas on Straight Street in the city of the Divine Silent Sackcloth Weaver. It was there that his mind would be changed, and his blinded eyes would be opened. Among those he intended to apprehend, Ananias, whose name means "God has been gracious," would pray and seek God's intervention for the restoration of Saul's sight. The name Judas, means "praise," therefore, Saul was taken to a house of praise.

In the lake of fire, Saul finds grace, not eternal damnation, or annihilation. Why? For this adversary, the lake is not a permanent destination; it is merely a transition phase. Paul emerged from it to become God's chief apostle. His initial place of darkness transforms into a house of praise, because the impurities and dross of an enemy were removed, fulfilling the promise we found in Isaiah 1:24-25.

Notice how Jesus meets us right where we are. He met Saul right where he was, on the road to Damascus, with a mindset under the covenant of the law. As Jesus told the Scribes and Pharisees, that covenant would bring darkness and death because of our inability to keep it. Just like us, Saul needed grace. On this road, Jesus gave Saul garments associated with the law, but promised to take him to a new destination, where he would exchange the sackcloth for garments of praise. Under the new covenant of God's grace, the sackcloth weaver's role would go silent. At the new place, there would not be a need for mourning, because Saul's sins were removed. There, he was saved by grace and his mindset straightened.

His new name, Paul, signifies "small or little." He was rendered small, or humbled, during his time of tribulation. It is noteworthy that the term "tribulation" is derived from the Greek word "thlipsis," meaning "to press" and is associated with the pressing of grapes in a winepress. Romans 2:9 (Nestle-Aland) further underscores this connection: "There will be tribulation (pressing) and distress for every human being who does evil, the Jew first and also the Greek." The Greek word for anguish, or distress, means "placed in a small space" – the winepress. This implies there is no more room for mental maneuvering. Jesus had revealed Himself. It was undeniable; it was over; it was finished.

This is precisely what occurred with Mr. Small – I mean Paul. Furthermore, Revelation 7:14 reads: "These are the ones who came out of the great tribulation (pressing, being made small), and they have washed their robes and made them white in the blood of the Lamb" (RSV). How can we miss this? There are too many coincidences in Paul's story to ignore the pointing toward a former enemy of the House of Israel taken through the fire of God's judgment with a good end on the other side of it. The fire and the brimstone did their jobs well.

Now, for additional evidence, let's apply some mathematical principles to what we learned in chapter 3 from Moses. In this analysis, I will convert the days between the major feast celebrations, as provided by Moses, to God's timetable. Here is the breakdown:

1. In God's timing, *"a day is as a thousand years, and a thousand years is as a day."*
2. On the calendar of Moses, 50 days represents the time between the first and second harvest. But that same time period was also referenced as a 1000-year period, when the first group rules and reigns. It is as *a day* to God.
3. Therefore, the 50-day period on the calendar of Moses, can be 1000 years on God's calendar, or it can also be as **a day**. I will use this "day" measurement, where 50 days on the calendar of Moses can represent **a day** on God's calendar.

Remember the 125 days between the second and third harvests on Moses' calendar? This period symbolized the time His enemies spent in outer darkness, the second death, before their harvest as grapes, signifying their resurrection. When converted to God's timetable, 1/50th of 125 days is 2.5, or 3 days. Saul, exemplifying how God treats His former enemies, spent 3 days in outer darkness and shame before the Holy Spirit descended like fire, transforming him into the new man, Paul. He was resurrected to a new life, and after the Holy Spirit fell upon him, he began speaking words that were previously unutterable to him. It was the language of praise to Jesus who had forgiven him and removed his sin.

Please note that according to Jewish custom, any part of a day is counted as a whole day, as exemplified in Jesus' case, where it was stated that He was in the tomb for three days and three nights. If He died on Friday afternoon and rose again on Sunday morning, then Friday, Saturday, and Sunday would be considered full days, adhering to the Jewish counting method. Similarly, 2.5 days for Saul in outer darkness, would be treated as "3 days."

The transformation and restoration of Saul align perfectly with Jesus' words to Nicodemus in John 3:1-16 (NASB):

> 1 Now there was a man of the Pharisees, named Nicodemus, a ruler of the Jews; 2. this man came to Jesus by night and said to Him, "Rabbi, we know that You have come from God as a teacher; for no one can do these signs that You do unless God is with him." 3. Jesus answered and said to him, "Truly, truly, I say to you, unless one is born again he cannot see the kingdom of God." 4. Nicodemus said to Him, "How can a man be born when he is old? He cannot enter a second time into his mother's womb and be born, can he?" 5. Jesus answered, "Truly, truly, I say to you, unless one is born of water and the Spirit he cannot enter into the kingdom of God." 6. "That which is born of the flesh is flesh, and that which is born of the Spirit is spirit." 7. "Do not be amazed that I said to you, 'You must be born again.' 8. "The wind blows where it wishes and you hear the sound of it, but do not know where it comes from and where it is going; so is everyone who is born of the Spirit." 9. Nicodemus said to Him, "How can these things be?" 10.

Jesus answered and said to him, "Are you the teacher of Israel, and do not understand these things?" 11. "Truly, truly, I say to you, we speak that which we know, and bear witness of that which we have seen; and you do not receive our witness." 12. "If I told you earthly things and you do not believe, how shall you believe if I tell you heavenly things?" 13. "And no one has ascended into heaven, but He who descended from heaven, even the Son of Man." 14. "And as Moses lifted up the serpent in the wilderness, even so must the Son of Man be lifted up; 15. that whoever believes may in Him have eternal life." 16. "For God so loved the world, that He gave His only begotten Son, that whoever believes in Him should not perish, but have eternal life."

Recorded conversations have played a crucial role in the transmission of God's Word throughout history. In this highly enlightening discussion, we gain another glimpse into God's heart. This intimate dialogue includes John 3:16, arguably the most famous and frequently quoted scripture in the Bible, found towards the end of the exchange where Jesus addresses questions about rebirth and inclusion in God's Kingdom.

Before we delve into this thought-provoking conversation, it would be beneficial to peer into the heart and mind of Nicodemus prior to this scene. His background provides significant insight, and the unfolding events leading up to that fateful night suggest a man burdened with a weary heart and a troubled conscience.

The late William Barclay did a masterful job discussing Nicodemus's background in Volume I of his commentary on the Gospel of John. First, Barclay points out that Nicodemus was likely a wealthy man, as indicated by John 19:39, which states that he brought a large mixture of myrrh and aloes for Jesus's body after His death – an act only feasible for someone affluent.

Second, the use of the Greek term "ruler" suggests that Nicodemus was a member of the Sanhedrin, the Supreme Court of the Jews. While their authority was somewhat limited under Roman rule, it remained substantial. On page 123, Barclay notes, "The Sanhedrin had jurisdiction over every Jew in the world, and one of its duties was to examine and deal with anyone suspected to be a false prophet."

Lastly, we are aware that Nicodemus was a Pharisee. As per Barclay, the Pharisees constituted an exclusive brotherhood whose members vowed to meticulously observe the scribal law until death. Expanding on this, Barclay provides detailed commentary on what it signified to be a member of the Pharisees on page 123. The very name "Pharisees" translated to "the Separated Ones," as they had chosen to set themselves apart from ordinary Jewish life to adhere to the law in every meticulous detail. The implications of this separation are outlined on pages 120-122, from which I have extracted the following information.

The Law, comprising the first five books of the Old Testament, held unparalleled sanctity for the Jews. It was deemed "the most sacred thing in the entire world," representing the "perfect word of God." Any attempt to "add one word to it or take one word away" was considered a "deadly sin." Beyond its foundational principles, described as "great, wide, noble principles" that individuals had to comprehend, the Law also established the finest guidelines for leading a virtuous life.

However, for the Jews of the later period, particularly those in Jesus's era, these foundational principles proved insufficient. They extracted from the Law an "infinite number of rules and regulations to govern every conceivable situation in life." In doing so, they transformed the law's grand principles into the legalism of detailed by-laws and regulations.

Barclay argues that this phenomenon is best illustrated by examining the Sabbath law. Rather than adhering to the straightforward biblical directive for a man and his household to keep the Sabbath holy and refrain from work, the Jews in this later period went on to produce twenty-four chapters of codified scribal law, meticulously defining work and detailing what activities were deemed lawful or unlawful on the Sabbath. Additionally, they devised methods to circumvent the prohibition of traveling on the Sabbath day (Exodus 16:29) by extending it to a two-thousand-cubit limitation for a Sabbath day's journey. Indeed, under scribal law, not only were rules and regulations extensive, but also the "evasions piled up by the hundred and the thousand." It is precisely this multiplication of scribal law that the Pharisees had committed to follow throughout their lives. We speculate that this inclination to develop an additional body of tradition beyond the Scriptures may have prompted Jesus's rebuke of the Pharisees, as documented in Matthew 23:24 (RSV), "You blind guides, straining out a gnat and swallowing a camel!"

Certainly, these Pharisees likely believed they were faithfully following all these laws and regulations. This self-perception might explain their irritation with Jesus, who consistently highlighted their continual failure to meet God's standard. Jesus's straightforward language would ultimately have fatal consequences for our Lord. Outward self-righteousness set them apart from their contemporaries, and pride emerged as a by-product of their legalism.

Here is the crux of the matter: the paramount principles of the law became overshadowed by the trivial details of their tradition. Their preoccupation with the literal interpretation of the law led them to overlook the underlying spirit. In fact, they were so blind that they failed to recognize the arrival of their own Messiah.

Nevertheless, it is crucial to grasp why it was so vital for the Pharisees to adhere to the law. Fulfilling it was not just about leading a virtuous life on earth; it also carried eternal consequences. According to Josephus, the Pharisees taught a resurrection:

> "That every soul is imperishable, but that only those of the righteous pass into another body, while those of the wicked are, on the contrary, punished with eternal torment" (Josephus Wars 2.8.14.) "They held the belief that an immortal strength belongs to souls, and that there are beneath the earth punishments and rewards for those who in life devoted themselves to virtue or vileness, and that eternal imprisonment is appointed for the latter, but the possibility of returning to life for the former" (Josephus Ant. 18.1.3).

The Sadducees could not embrace this line of thinking as these concepts were absent from the Torah. This disparity led to a division between the two groups. The Pharisees propagated the idea that access to God's Kingdom hinged on an individual's righteousness, implying that eternal life awaited those who fulfilled the law. Moreover, the Pharisees anticipated a day when the current evil age would be eradicated, and the righteous kingdom of Israel would be instituted. They held the belief that their own righteousness would pave the way for the Messiah to inaugurate this kingdom.

To say there was much at stake in their ability to fulfill the law would be an understatement. Adherence to the law not only promised a better life on earth but also ensured eternal security in the life to come. For a devoted Pharisee like Nicodemus, the burden of this responsibility must have been overwhelming.

How could one determine if they were righteous enough? The law became the measuring stick, and for Pharisees who were intellectually honest, their inability to fully adhere to it likely weighed heavily on their conscience. Such was the legacy of Nicodemus as a Pharisee.

We should also note the intriguing timeline of this conversation. The book of John primarily centers around the events leading up to the Crucifixion. For instance, consider the cleansing of the Temple, which stands as perhaps the most dramatic confrontation between Jesus and religious orthodoxy outside of His trial and execution. In this incident, He expelled money changers and those selling cattle, sheep, and doves from the temple. This event was the most significant tax-collecting occasion of the year for the Jewish leadership, and there's nothing quite as likely to get a person in trouble as interfering with someone else's pursuit of money. Yet, Jesus boldly entered the Temple, likely overturning every table in sight. This story is documented in John chapter 2, whereas the other Gospels placed this event near the conclusion of their respective accounts.

A documentary on the History Channel a few years ago suggested that this incident at the Temple sealed our Lord's fate in the eyes of Jewish authorities. Until then, Jesus had only been a thorn in their side, but by disrupting their financial operations, He had pushed their tolerance beyond the breaking point. Removing Jesus would have taken on a new level of urgency.

Simultaneously, the Roman rulers of Judea were struggling to maintain the approval of their overseers in the Roman White House. Some of their fellow politicians were questioning their ability to govern and maintain peace. Consequently, both Herod and Pilate might have feared that any disturbance, such as the one caused by Jesus on the most significant religious and financial day of the year, had the potential to attract further unwanted attention.

Eliminating this agitator, from both the Jewish and Roman perspectives, would have presented an easy solution. Consequently, religious and civil authorities reached an agreement on how to deal with this troublesome rabbi. The circumstances were now ripe for His execution. Enter Nicodemus – a wealthy, well-educated aristocrat, esteemed and respected in the community as a Pharisee and a member of the Jewish Supreme Court.

Why did this highly regarded man feel the need to approach Jesus at night? Perhaps the answer lies in his awareness as a powerful insider. It is likely that he was keenly aware of his colleagues' intense hostility and their plans to destroy Him. However, we also know that he believed Jesus to be a man of God.

This internal conflict must have caused considerable stress in his mind. Perhaps he felt he could be the voice of reason amidst all the emotional chaos. Apparently, there were other Pharisees who felt the same way, but they were evidently not in control. For instance, some of them even warned Jesus of an attempt on his life: "On that very day some Pharisees came, saying to Him, 'Get out and depart from here, for Herod wants to kill you'" (Luke 13:31, NKJV).

As a member of the Supreme Court, we are certain that Nicodemus had adjudicated in numerous challenging situations. Perhaps he felt he could apply his skills to find a rational way to alleviate the tension between this revered teacher and his own party. Meeting at night would guarantee privacy for their conversation, which would not be easily achievable in a public setting during daylight with tempers running high and the atmosphere already poisoned with hatred. At night, Nicodemus could speak from his heart without fearing his peers who were ready to lash out in anger.

Nicodemus's initial statements to Jesus appeared sincere and respectful, recognizing Him as a teacher from God and, more significantly, as someone "with God." Jesus discerned the inner conflict within Nicodemus's mind, understanding the turmoil in his heart and the origin of the tension within his soul—how could a man of God be in such conflict with other men of God?

Jesus directly addressed the matter in verse 3: "Truly, truly, I say to you, unless one is born again, he cannot see the kingdom of God." In other words, only a person who is born again can be truly "with God."

Many believe Nicodemus had no idea what Jesus meant by "born again." However, this was far from the case; Nicodemus understood perfectly. Jesus employed a phrase well-known to both the Jews and Greeks of the first century. The expression "born again" signified a radical and transformative change.

According to Barclay, as mentioned on page 126 of his commentary on John, Jews during the New Testament era were acquainted with the concept of rebirth. Rabbis taught that a pagan proselyte converting to Judaism became equivalent to a newborn infant. Sins committed before conversion were expunged, and it was even theoretically argued that such a person "could marry his own mother or sister, because he was a completely new man..."

Simultaneously, the most prevalent religions for the Greeks and Romans during this era were the mystery religions. These religions were all "founded on the story of some suffering, dying, and rising god." A key element of these mystery religions was a mystical union with the relevant deity. Upon achieving this union through various rites, the initiate was, in the language of the Mysteries, considered "twice-born."

Consequently, many of these mystery religions emphasized the significance of regeneration in the salvation of their followers. The Roman satirist and philosopher Apuleius asserted that through "a voluntary death" in initiation, he had undergone a "spiritual birthday" and had been reborn.

Other symbols of rebirth included midnight initiation ceremonies and the consumption of milk. The most renowned of all Mystery ceremonies was the taurobolium, or bull-slaying ritual of the Mithras cult. Without going into further details about this rebirth ceremony, it is noteworthy that the taurobolium was depicted in one of the scenes in an HBO series titled "Rome." If HBO could gather information about these rebirth ceremonies, how probable is it that an educated man like Nicodemus was aware of them in his time?

The conclusive evidence that Nicodemus comprehended the meaning of Jesus' phrase "you must be born again" lies in his response: "How can a man be born again when he is old?" If he hadn't grasped the concept, his question would likely have been, "How can any man be born again?" The historical record and the language used in the text serve as evidence that Nicodemus understood Jesus perfectly. And why wouldn't he? Jesus had no reason to confuse him.

Equipped with this understanding, we can now discern that Jesus was communicating clearly in a deeply personal conversation with Nicodemus.

Jesus was calling for a profound transformation, and from Nicodemus's response, we see that it resonated with something deep within his soul.

At this point, he could have been greatly offended. After all, he was an esteemed man who had humbled himself, taking the initiative as a peacemaker to approach Jesus with an offer of reconciliation. However, Nicodemus was not offended; instead, he felt convicted.

Jesus had pinpointed the source of discomfort. Barclay comments: "It is not the desirability of change that Nicodemus questioned; it is the possibility. Nicodemus was up against the eternal problem, the problem of the man who wants to be changed and who cannot change himself."

Please note the natural flow of the conversation, Nicodemus' reaction to the perceived impossibility, and how Jesus responded in love. After Nicodemus recognized the problem, Jesus replied like a loving father, teacher, and friend. He reiterated the need for change, acknowledged the flesh's inability to accomplish it, and pointed to the power of the Spirit as the only solution: "Truly, truly, I say to you, unless one is born of water and the Spirit, he cannot enter into the kingdom of God."

In essence, that which is born of the flesh is limited [unable], and that which is born of the Spirit is empowered [more than able]. Entry into God's Kingdom would be based on the grace of God through the power of the Spirit. A person by themselves is constrained by the weakness of the flesh, a universal fact of human experience! However, the essence of the Spirit is power and life.

Jesus then drew a parallel between the Spirit's role in rebirth and the unpredictable nature of the wind. Rebirth occurs when the Spirit imparts a portion of Himself, granting the person the ability to believe. He then reminded Nicodemus that man does not control the wind. No one knows where the wind comes from or where it goes. The wind (Spirit) blows where it wills! Just as no child has control over when, where, or how they will be born, a person has no control over the wind.

This was Jesus' response regarding the concept of being born again. The conversation could have concluded at this juncture, as he provided the singular and definitive answer. If one were to diagram the rebirth process, there would not be a decision diamond involving Nicodemus. The one overseeing this process is the Spirit, identified as the Father, and all decisions pertaining to birth rest with Him.

Jesus did not find it necessary to elaborate further, but his response to Nicodemus was truly surprising. Naturally, Nicodemus had more questions, given that the Lord's answer sharply contrasted with what he had been taught throughout his life. Nicodemus responded to Jesus' words much like contemporary Christians might react if they were as perceptive as he was: "How can that be?"

Once again, Jesus provided a clear response to this question. Beginning in verse 14, he recounted a familiar, yet unusual, Old Testament story about Moses lifting up a serpent in the wilderness. In this narrative, God unleashed fiery serpents upon the people due to their disobedience. Many perished, while others fell ill and faced impending death. The Lord then instructed Moses in Numbers 21:8 (KJV), saying: "Make a fiery serpent, and set it upon a pole; and it shall come to pass, that every one that is bitten, when he looketh upon it, shall live."

Jesus, in a parallel manner, became the accursed One lifted up on a tree for the purpose of rescuing, healing, and restoring. Pay close attention to the precise wording: "It shall come to pass." Our Father has ordained that those bitten by the metaphorical snake will experience healing when they witness what the Savior accomplished on the Cross.

In "A Generous Orthodoxy," Brian McLaren, the founding pastor of Cedar Ridge Community Church in Baltimore, conveyed the idea that in the Bible, the term 'save' denotes 'rescue' or 'heal.' Its interpretation may vary across passages, but generally, it signifies 'getting out of trouble' in any given context.

Lastly, Jesus made an "extra point" by explaining the "why" behind God's willingness to provide salvation to mankind. John 3:16 commences with the conjunction "For" or "Because." According to the text, we understand that He did it out of love, ensuring our safe entry into His Kingdom and presence. Jeremiah 18:1-6 reinforces what Jesus taught Nicodemus:

> "1. The word which came to Jeremiah from the LORD, saying, 2. Arise, and go down to the potter's house, and there I will cause thee to hear my words. 3. Then I went down to the potter's house, and, behold, he wrought a work on the wheels. 4. And the vessel that he made of clay was marred in the hand of the potter: so he made it again

another vessel, as seemed good to the potter to make it. 5. Then the word of the LORD came to me, saying, 6. O house of Israel, cannot I do with you as this potter? saith the LORD. Behold, as the clay is in the potter's hand, so are ye in mine hand, O house of Israel" (KJV).

Darroll Evans, wrote a wonderful article entitled "Life in the Potter's House." Here are a few excerpts that summarize what Jesus taught Nicodemus:

"Jeremiah 18:1-6 is the classic Biblical story of clay in the hands of the Master Potter. That analogy is used throughout the Bible. As in dealing with pottery, the "throw" has been made, and the clay is on the wheel. The Old and New Testaments represent separate "throws" ... In Verse 6, God asks Israel, *Can't I do with you as the Potter in the story has done with his clay? After all, you are My clay, in My hands, even as the physical clay is molded in the hands of the human potter.* The response to God's inquiry is obvious! ... Clay in the hands of the Master Potter can be done with as He pleases. Isaiah 64:8 (KJV) *"But now, O LORD, thou art our Father; we are the clay, and thou our potter; and we all are the work of thy hand."* This verse is plain, blunt, and obvious to even the casual reader. "We are the clay, and God is the Potter; we are the work of His hands." However, human ego often rejects such a perspective. Despite attempting to mold ourselves, it proves unsuccessful, leading us astray. In fact, our self-directed efforts are inherently flawed. In the Old Testament, the clay was marred, illustrating the impracticality of a works-oriented salvation or self-molding. So, the Potter took another "throw" and initiated the process of remaking the vessel. This time, in the New Testament, the clay took the form of grace. It was on the Cross that salvation by works was eliminated."

This should have been excellent news for Nicodemus—knowing that he did not have to depend on his own works to enter God's Kingdom. This is precisely how and why Jesus could transform Saul, a former adversary of the House of Israel, into the honorable vessel we witness in Paul. When Saul raised his eyes and realized he was conversing with the accursed One lifted up on the Cross, the process of rebirth commenced. Within three days, he experienced a transformative rebirth; he was healed. It was a baptism by fire. His experience served as the "pattern" of how Jesus brings about a radical change in the life of a former enemy.

According to 1 Corinthians 12:3, it is declared that no one can say 'Jesus is Lord' except by the Holy Spirit, and this includes Paul, after being filled by it. Moreover, Philippians 2:10-11 (RSV) articulates: "that at the name of Jesus every knee should bow, in heaven and on earth and under the earth, and every tongue confess that Jesus Christ is Lord, to the glory of God the Father." Regrettably, most widely used translations, like the one here, substitute the word "should" for "shall" in this passage. The use of "should" implies that individuals like Saul ought to bow and confess, but might not choose to do so.

However, due to our Lord's passionate love, verse 10 commences with the Greek word "Hina," translated as "That." This word signifies "in order that," or "so that." According to BAGD (a Biblical Greek dictionary), Dr. Daniel Wallace, and others, the use of "hina" here "indicates the intention **and its sure accomplishment**." God's love for enemies, such as Saul, cannot be quenched.

This assurance is echoed in John 3:16 – "that (hina) whosoever believeth in Him, '**should** not perish but have everlasting life' (KJV)? No, it is '**shall** not perish but have everlasting life.' The structure of this purpose-result clause is designed to convey that what God purposes is what happens, expressing divine purpose and the definite end result. There is no uncertainty regarding the fate of the believer in John 3:16, just as there is no question about what Saul would experience.

Moreover, the term translated as "confess" is "exomologeo." In all other instances where this term or a form of it is used, the act of confessing is done willingly. For instance, in Luke 10:21 (RSV), Jesus employed this word to confess with thanksgiving: "I thank thee, Father." This aligns with Paul's expression of gratitude when he willingly confesses that Jesus is his Lord. Paul is not just confessing; he is grateful and joyous to be liberated from his former state of darkness and death under the law.

Similarly, all others from the first two resurrections will experience joy and amazement when they celebrate the deliverance of former enemies from the third harvest. While there might be some initial hesitation about trusting a former enemy, as seen in the believers' reaction during Paul's conversion, their concerns are resolved when they learn that Jesus has "justified" or "certified" their transformation. This realization allows everyone to relax and revel in God's victory.

10

The Three Heavens
and the unutterable things
that can now be told

I BELIEVE WHEN those in the last group are resurrected from death to life, it will be one of the greatest celebrations in the history of mankind. The foreshadowing of this event is presented in our Lord's first miracle, and it is laden with symbolic connections to the third group. Those links cannot be easily be dismissed.

As we know, this inaugural miracle, His number one miracle, unfolded at a wedding in Cana, where Jesus transformed water into wine. Those who tasted the wine remarked that the bridegroom had departed from the custom of the day, **saving** the best for the **last**. I interpret this initial act in His ministry as a foreshadowing of what humanity will consider to be His finest work—the salvation of those in the third group, the last ones. It seems He was indicating that during His future wedding celebration, where He is the Bridegroom, He will transform those grapes into a remarkable vintage.

Recall the imagery of the holy city descending as His Bride in Revelation 21:2 – "And I saw the holy city, new Jerusalem, coming down from God out of heaven, prepared as a bride adorned for her husband" (RSV). Those outside the city, in outer darkness experiencing the lake of fire, will witness Jesus, the Bridegroom, deviating from the custom of the day (the law) and extending grace to those former enemies. Also, bear in mind how God's messenger, Jesus, demonstrated power over fire and issued the command to harvest the grapes in Revelation chapter 14.

During His number one miracle, we learn that He transformed all six containers of ordinary water (substance from a lake) into the finest wine, and this remarkable event took place on the third day of the wedding feast – **the third feast day!** Additionally, in biblical symbolism, the number "six" represents mankind, human weakness, and the presence of sin. Jesus, as promised on the third feast day, undertakes a transformation, justification, or fixing of these symbolic elements.

Revelation chapter 14 further enlightens us about the location of the winepress, situated outside the city. This winepress serves to remove the flesh of the grapes when Jesus places His enemies under His feet, producing a wonderful byproduct. The extensive use of symbolic language and imagery in these passages all points to the third harvest and its corresponding celebration.

Interestingly, Jesus performed His first recorded healing in Cana. In John 4:46-54, a nobleman from Herod Antipas's court seeks Jesus for the healing of his son, who resides outside the city of Cana in Capernaum. Concerning Capernaum, Jesus once declared, "And thou, Capernaum, which art exalted unto heaven, shalt be brought down to hell (Hades): for if the mighty works, which have been done in thee, had been done in Sodom, it would have remained until this day" (Matthew 11:23, KJV).

The state of Capernaum seems to parallel Israel's historical journey. In that place in Hades, the grave, the nobleman's son was in a state of death, "burning up" with fever. From the city where Jesus turned water into wine, He pronounced healing for the boy. We then learn that the healing occurred at the seventh hour, symbolizing the last day in God's creation story when everything is pronounced "good." This moment signifies God finishing His work and humanity entering the day of God's rest. At this point, the nobleman's entire family, residents of Capernaum, embraced belief.

Speaking of healing or saving people on the seventh day, Jesus performed healing miracles on the Sabbath several times (I have counted at least four, possibly five). His actions irked the Pharisees, who believed it was not in alignment with God's plan to **heal on the Sabbath, the seventh day of rest. These religious leaders deemed it "unlawful," going beyond the boundaries of God's will and law.** This belief and attitude sounds too familiar. To me, only a sick mind would consider healing and restoring someone **at any time** as a bad idea, and that includes restoration after the second resurrection. However, Jesus responded more gracefully than I. (I am still a work-in-progress.)

During one of those occasions in Luke 6:8-11, the passage informs us that Jesus discerned the thoughts of the Pharisees, and here is how He responded to this distorted way of thinking: He asked the Pharisees in verse 9 (KJV): "Is it lawful on the Sabbath days to do good, or to do evil? **To save life, or to destroy it?**" I am sure there was some silence, like what might be occurring now, as the resurrection of the third group is considered. Then, He healed the man, and the Pharisees "were filled with madness."

If Jesus were to rescue someone from outer darkness and give them life, would we be mad, sad, or glad? I believe we would be ecstatic! It would be a celebration like no other.

In the Bible, the number "3" signifies "divine completeness and perfection." Hope Bolinger, in an article on Crosswalk.com, enhances our understanding of the number three with these insights: "The number three appears in the Bible 467 times, fewer than the number seven, but more than most of the other symbolically important numbers. Sometimes three is used as an emphatic Semitic triplet to describe the intensity of something. It's not just holy. It's holy, holy, holy."

Hope referred to Revelation 4:8, where the phrase "holy, holy, holy" is found. In that chapter, the four living creatures, symbolic of those in the second resurrection, are singing and giving praise to the Lord. When this group starts singing these words, the elders, representing those ruling and reigning from the first resurrection, who are clad in white garments with golden crowns on their heads, cast down their crowns. Why? Because this signifies the end of the millennium and the thousand-year reign.

In the following chapter, John observes these two groups together again around the throne, and then he hears in verse 13: "every creature in heaven and on earth and under the earth and in the sea and all therein" giving praise and honor to Jesus (Nestle-Aland). This view is evidently after the third and final harvest, signifying that our God has declared each group, "HOLY!"

As a side note, I believe the 144,000 symbolizes the first group while they lived their lives on earth before their resurrection. In the 7th chapter, notice how they are not harmed UNTIL they have been sealed. Later, they are portrayed as elders after their resurrection, ruling and reigning until the rest of the dead are raised.

In summary, we have identified three groups of people, three harvests, three crops, and three vivifications at three distinct times. All of these are associated with the three different feast celebrations. Consequently, we can now gain a better understanding of what Paul meant when he said he was caught up to the third heaven—a "holy, holy, holy" place.

What distinguishes these three heavens? For most of my life, I thought of them solely in spatial terms, possibly stacked on top of each other, with Jesus residing in the upper section. Then, during a local radio show about growing the best crops in your garden, the host caught my attention with an often-repeated phrase: **"You can't improve upon perfection!"** He was referring to the produce a garden would yield if you followed his instructions.

That got me thinking—maybe each heaven is the same perfect place. Then, it dawned on me: the only difference between them is the size of their population. When I revisited the scriptures, a close friend pointed out what I had missed all those years—this perspective was not just about a place; it was also about timing and purpose. The Greek word translated as "to" in the phrase "caught up to the third heaven" is a preposition that signifies movement toward a place, time, or purpose.

I am now convinced that Paul was caught up to a place we call paradise, at a time after the third harvest, when God's purpose had been fulfilled—when He had become "all in all." The only distinction between each heaven was the size of its population after each harvest.

There were no neon signs flashing "THIRD HEAVEN, THIRD HEAVEN, THIRD HEAVEN" when Paul arrived, nor an angelic elevator operator announcing an arrival on the third floor with its fine selections of wine. Paul called it the third heaven because he saw and heard people from the third harvest, alongside all others in heaven from the first two harvests, praising Him with great joy (Luke 15:7). Below are some details to confirm what I have stated.

In 2 Corinthians 12, Paul states that a man was caught up to the third heaven and heard things that cannot be told—things that it is not possible, permissible, or lawful for "a man" to speak. Here, Paul used the third person to tell this story as "a man," reinforcing what he had said at the beginning of the chapter—namely, this man, Paul, **was going to boast of things that showed his weakness!**

In verse 3, Paul mentioned that he knew or remembered this man from the past, and one writer described the relaying of Paul's story as having an "apologetic" tone. Having just boasted about his weakness in a previous narrative, he declared his intention to do it again at the beginning of his second story. Subsequently, he stated that there was nothing to gain from it, emphasizing that it merely displayed another former weakness of his.

Moving to verse 5, Paul asserted that he would boast **concerning what happened to him**, but he would not boast in himself, except in his weakness. So, what is Paul's weakness in this story? And why aren't we looking for it? It is essential to emphasize that he initiated the chapter with the words, "I must boast."

For many, including myself, the allure of the mystical things he heard that cannot be revealed to us mere mortals was the focus of my attention. Thus, I was not actively seeking the boasting in his weakness until now— over 50 years after the first time I read it. Talk about weakness—I believe mine surpasses Paul's.

Furthermore, what could be so extraordinary about heaven that speaking about it would be deemed "unlawful"? We've already been informed that the saved will be resurrected from the dead, forgiven, and granted immortality and a new body. There will be no more pain, suffering, or tears. For those more inclined toward worldly pleasures, there will be mansions, streets of gold, pearly gates, and, for someone like me, hopefully, golf, good wine, and Blue Bell Ice Cream.

What else could we desire or need, and what makes all this goodness "unlawful" to speak about? And who told Paul that what he heard was unlawful for "a man" (**referring to his former self**) to speak about? Was it the elevator operator, an angel, or Jesus? The text does not directly inform us. Perhaps Paul did not find it necessary to specify, because it was so evident to him that his former self, with his Pharisaic training, considered what he heard as unlawful to speak about, even as a possibility!

"Unlawful" refers to something not conforming to, recognized by, or in harmony with the law. I propose that it was grace that was not in harmony with the works of the law. For a Pharisee, the notion of a former enemy in heaven was unthinkable – unutterable! It may have been unspeakable even in Paul's mind during his early years of training as a new Christian. That was the weakness he was boasting about! Justifying the ungodly by God's gracious acts alone was not in harmony with a man's work under the law (Romans 4:5), nor with a man's ego and desire to be self-sufficient and autonomous – to be his own god. This was Paul's weakness going into the vision—an incomplete knowledge of God's grace.

Paul was just like us. He did not receive a complete understanding of all scriptures on the first day of his conversion. He had to learn, as any person would. Were you born with your present knowledge, or did you have to struggle—read, study, ask, and pray? This is why Paul said he knew that man from "fourteen years ago."

Paul had preconceived notions burned into his brain too—stuff that he needed to get rid of. He was "a man" in this vision; he was that man! And believe it or not, we may have preconceived notions burned into our brains too; notions that need to be replaced and will be removed only by the light from a brilliant heavenly Father.

So, what did Paul hear when he was caught up to the third heaven? I am thoroughly convinced that he heard God's former enemies, after the fire of the Holy Spirit fell upon them, giving praise and thanksgiving to the One who saved them by His grace. According to his old self, that was not possible; it was unthinkable, therefore, unspeakable, or unutterable.

How do we know what Paul heard? Here is the big clue – The idea of speaking in tongues, after the Holy Spirit falls on a person, was always strange to me. But maybe it was meant to be strange. Perhaps it is a foreshadowing of a significant event in mankind's future that would sound strange to our human way of thinking. Maybe it is what happens at the third harvest when the unthinkable occurs, when His former enemies are justified by His grace, not by their works. And with this new revelation, they start praising Him for it!

When the Holy Spirit, part of the Godhead associated with the third group, falls as fire on them, they start speaking sincere words of praise directly to our Father (1 Corinthians 14:2), words they previously could not express. Before this awakening, they had no understanding of His unmerited favor. But after their harvest, they will comprehend it completely—by experience. These words of praise are like a foreign language to them. It is also currently foreign to the thinking of many, because it teaches that God will save what they think is unsavable, doing what they consider is impossible **during the seventh day of rest.**

There is a popular song on the radio that we sang at a church I recently attended – "Unstoppable God." The words fit so well, proclaiming that mercy is triumphant on the **third day**, because nothing is impossible for Him, and no one is going to stop Him. The passion in the fire of His love is unquenchable!

Here, Paul is boasting about his previous lack of knowledge. But miraculously, by the power of God in a stunning vision, he came to a new understanding. Grace may have been a possibility in the back of Paul's mind, based on his experience during his early training as a Christian, but now he would receive confirmation and confidence from above.

With this knowledge, let us go back to the first story, where he began the boasting. There, Paul was facing a life-and-death situation, and God provided a window of hope. In that story, there was a wall, a barrier, with death on one side, and life on the other.

I submit that the wall of separation was like the covenant of the law. Death was on the side where Paul once found himself, because of his inability to keep it. Paul then escaped death in the basket of Grace, attached to a rope – his lifeline to freedom – Jesus! Our Savior provided the basket, and He was the rope that took all the stress in bringing Paul to life! We, like Paul, are simply along for the ride in His basket of unmerited favor.

I believe the weakness in the first story was a setup for how Paul would describe his former weakness in the second. I also do not think that we, in the 21st century, can possibly understand how huge of a change this was for an Israelite. Paul needed this confirmation of being caught up to the third heaven to be able to carry out his mission, even unto his death.

My friend, Clyde Pilkington, wrote: "This special gospel committed specifically and singularly to Paul (thus, 'my gospel') stands in contrast to the law. It is this good news that God will one day use as the standard to judge the world (Romans 2:16.)"

For those who have not yet apprehended the third harvest, the thought of enemies being forgiven and justified is unutterable to them. Perhaps they will have to wait and experience the third heaven before their eyes are finally opened – just as it was in the case of Paul.

But God is not worried or frustrated by His kids' temporary lack of knowledge. He knew in advance how His people might temporarily miss this good news, and He predicted our dilemma when He told the Church through Paul in Ephesians 2:7-9: "in the ages to come (the future) He will show (by action because of our poor understanding now) the exceeding riches (beyond what was expected – a third harvest – the grapes) of His grace in kindness towards us in Christ Jesus. For by grace (unmerited favor) you have been saved (harvested) through faith, and that not of yourselves; it is the gift of God, not of works, lest anyone should boast" (KJV).

We, the barley, wheat, and grapes, are His workmanship. We were created in Christ Jesus for good works, which God previously arranged in the harvests for us to walk in them. Crops are crops by His design; it is the natural order of things. It is in the plant's DNA to be who they are, and no amount of effort by the plant can change its identity. That is why there will be no boasting! The fact is that He loves all of us, whether barley, wheat, or grape, and for that reason, He became the Savior of the world, the One who will harvest all the crops for His enjoyment and pleasure.

As Minister Phil Henry reminds us: "Behold, the lamb of God, who takes away the sin of the world was a proclamation – not an invitation; it was a declaration – not a negotiation; it is not something to be debated." When we finally acknowledge that our entry into God's kingdom was based on His decision and His righteousness, all forms of self-righteousness will be destroyed in a very small space as we discover this truth – His love was the catalyst for our salvation, and our confession was simply the end result.

Once mankind is finally able to see their place in God's plan, they will also see their role as He used all three of these groups to teach us the difference between good and evil, the difference between law and grace, and the difference between the old heavens and earth and the new ones, meant for us to enjoy in peace and harmony with each other. Paul was an example, a prototype, of how God treats His enemies and His long-term plans for them.

Maybe, this is why His Word tells us to love your enemies, do good to them, bless them, pray for them, feed them, give them drink, never bring vengeance, and do not rejoice when your enemy falls. Is God a hypocrite? Does He ask us to do something that He has no intentions of doing? No!

Our Lord's judgment of His enemy, Saul, was a signpost indicating the direction He is going with them. When all is said and done, I believe the barley will understand how they could have just as easily been a grape, and grapes could have just as easily been barley or wheat. In this, we will understand that vessels chosen for honor or dishonor in this short life had roles to play for the overall benefit of humanity's training, and He loved them all equally. As any good parent, God shows no favoritism nor partiality toward any of His offspring – Deuteronomy 10:17, 2 Chronicles 19:7, Acts 10:34, Romans 2:11, and Ephesians 6:9.

If God's expression of hatred towards Esau, in choosing one deceitful and unworthy brother over another unworthy brother, resulted in a lifetime of blessings for Esau, a restored relationship with his brother as described in Genesis 33:4, and ultimately culminated in the salvation of both in one of the three harvests, what does that convey about His love for Esau? What does it indicate about His love for both brothers, and by extension, His love for us?

I believe the stories of Jacob and Esau were crafted as object lessons illustrating humanity's universal need for grace, irrespective of our status in this life. Personally, there have been moments when my actions mirrored the characteristics of both brothers, as I am a sinner unworthy of His blessings and love, saved solely by His grace, and I continue to bask in it every day. How about you?

If God elected a man like Saul, who participated in the persecution of innocent followers of Jesus, a traitor to his own heritage, a Pharisee of Pharisees, and a proclaimed enemy of God, to be His chief apostle, over seemingly more honorable candidates, it was to underscore the reality that none of us are inherently righteous or deserving. God, being in control, took responsibility for all three harvests. Moreover, God foresaw that once humanity caught a glimpse of His grace, we would finally comprehend the kind of love He desires us to have for each other – unconditional love that is essential for experiencing everlasting peace and harmony.

Observe how God illustrated a perfect picture of grace for us in Daniel 9:27 – "And he shall confirm the covenant with many for one week; and in the midst of the week, he shall cause the sacrifice and oblation to cease, and for the overspreading of abominations, he shall make it desolate, even until the consummation, and that shall be poured upon the desolate" (KJV).

Five Hebrew words contribute to the phrase "And he shall confirm the covenant with many for one week." These words are: covenant, confirm, many, one, and week. Notably, this "one week" comes after the appearance of the Messiah at the conclusion of 69 weeks. It is reasonable to interpret this "one week" as referring to the final and 70th week.

While "covenant," "one," and "week" are adequately translated, let us explore alternatives for the words "confirm" and "many," which could potentially enhance our understanding. "Confirm" is fitting, but "strengthen" and "empower" are viable alternatives too. In the Septuagint, a Greek translation of the Old Testament, the Greek term used here is related to our English word for dynamite and is also employed by Paul to describe the Gospel as the power (dynamite) of God unto salvation.

So, how does one strengthen and empower the new covenant? (I am certain it was the new covenant of Grace that was being confirmed, strengthened, and empowered here, because the old covenant of the law was put to death in the middle of that last week, when the sacrifices ceased because of our Lord's death on the Cross.) What kind of strengthening would add power like dynamite to this new covenant?

Consider the notion that the covenant of unmerited favor was fortified by selecting individuals who fled and denied Him during His Crucifixion. Yet, a more profound example illustrates the extent of His grace – choosing an enemy, a Pharisee of Pharisees, a murder-condoning, hubristic figure feared by other followers of Jesus. That choice stands as grace on an extraordinary scale, almost like grace on steroids. Selecting someone like Saul would present a vivid portrayal of unmerited favor, conclusively affirming that the new covenant was solely about grace! This act served as a dynamic showcase (Romans 3:25, 26) of what grace truly entails, visible for all to witness.

Moreover, the Hebrew word translated as "many," in its adjective form, means "sufficient" and "enough." Both these terms aptly align with the narrative, as God strengthened the covenant of grace with a sufficient amount, or enough, to ensure the Word reached the world.

However, this Hebrew noun can also denote "chief." Consequently, Jesus might not have been exclusively referring to His small group of followers, but specifically to Paul. Supporting this, in 1 Timothy 1:15, Paul identifies himself as the "chief" among sinners.

The phrase "And in the midst of the week, he shall cause the sacrifice and oblation to cease" signifies the midpoint of the last week when Jesus, after His 3 ½ year ministry, was crucified, becoming the ultimate sacrifice that rendered all future sacrifices unnecessary.

Research indicates that the Damascus Road experience, marking Paul's conversion, occurred approximately 3 years after the Crucifixion.

Therefore, I propose that Paul's conversion transpired exactly 3 ½ years after the Crucifixion, symbolizing the conclusion of the 70 weeks.

This marked the calling of individuals, including Paul, "the chief among sinners," as the perfect embodiment of grace for humanity's contemplation. In this perspective, Paul's conversion represents the culmination of the 70 weeks. God, having adequately reinforced the visual representation of grace for historical reflection, chose a former enemy from His own household (Matthew 10:36) to spearhead the dissemination of the gospel of grace to the nations.

For a brief period, I believed I had a new understanding of this Daniel passage. However, after a few months, while reading a commentary on Bible Hub's web page, I discovered that others had previously suggested the end of the 70 weeks coincided with the calling of Paul. Although this concept is not a prerequisite for believing in the third resurrection, it is an intriguing thought worth considering.

Yet, there is another compelling example that should resonate even more deeply with you and me—our own stories! From personal experience, we intimately understand the essence of unmerited favor. Each of us can assert with certainty, "I am a sinner, loved by Jesus, and saved by His grace." This profound realization is uniquely ours.

Paul, in Romans, reflected that God's choice of you and me (predestination) was not based on our righteousness as compared to others, but was an exhibition of His greatest work—transforming vessels of wrath into vessels of mercy. Left with nothing more to do than marvel at His love, we become willing and humble servants participating in His magnificent plan of redemption for others.

In our training, vessels of honor and dishonor are easily shaped by reinforcing His presence in our lives, or succumbing to the delusion of His absence. Perhaps it is time to reconsider His enemies. When we encounter them, we might be looking at a reflection of who we are without His presence in our lives. His choice of them as vessels of dishonor might serve as training for us, as He molds and shapes us into His likeness. His desire is not only for us to discern the difference between good and evil, but to genuinely yearn for the good.

To change the mind of a former enemy, all it might take is His appearance to them, just as He did for Paul. In that moment, it's Game-Set-Match! Or, as Dr. Thomas Talbott would say, "Checkmate, game over!" God knows precisely when and how to reach each of us.

Meanwhile, "But God has chosen the foolish things of the world to confound the wise; and God has chosen the weak things of the world to confound the things which are mighty; and base things of the world, and things which are despised, has God chosen, yea, and things which are not, to bring to nought things that are: **that no flesh should glory in His presence**" 1 Corinthians 1:27-29, KJV).

Clyde Pilkington clarifies: "The Lord Jesus Christ was the Son of God, but the one who had the distinguished role of being His earthly 'father' was Joseph. A simple man, and from all earthly perception, he was what we might call an average 'Joseph' - or an average 'Joe.' He was a lowly carpenter, making our Lord the son of an average Joe. This was not an accident, for it is indeed our Father's method. The Father does not plan and build spiritual life upon social prestige, honor, respect, and position. He has made clear the divine method: 'For you see your calling, brethren, how that not many wise men after the flesh, not many mighty, not many noble, are called' (1 Corinthians 1:26, KJV)."

Recognizing God's unmerited favor on her, Mary responded perfectly with: "My soul magnifies the Lord, and my spirit rejoices in God my Savior, for He has regarded the low estate of His handmaiden. . . for He who is mighty has done great things for me, and holy is His name" (Luke 1:46-48, RSV).

Even in our weaknesses, we find encouraging words from Jesus to Peter in the last verses of John's gospel. Right after Peter's denial and admission that he did not have the right stuff to love Him with the sacrificial love he desired to possess, Jesus promised to develop him (make him into a rock). Jesus told him that in his old age, he would have the right kind of love to fulfill his calling. This example lets us know a little more about our Father's ability to mold and shape the clay into something better and stronger.

Peter must have been elated at that point, and then he asked the Lord about his close friend, John. Jesus replied that if He wanted John to remain alive until He returned, then it had nothing to do with Peter's destiny for martyrdom. The facts are that Peter was crucified, and John died of old age in Ephesus, the only apostle to die peacefully. Each had a calling, and each fulfilled his destiny in Christ as God designed, just like you and I will by relying on His strength and not our own.

One other note about Peter: It appears that he also needed some help in understanding our Lord's plan for three resurrections. So, Jesus gave him a vision of the three heavens. In that vision, a sheet full of unclean animals came down from heaven three different times, signifying the three groups that God cleanses. He then told Peter that what God has made clean, don't call unclean.

Question: Are we saying that people who are in the third group will be forever unclean? God's response might be: "You, who were once unclean, should not go there."

Furthermore, since God does not play favorites, then your story, when completed, will be one for the ages, just like Peter's, Paul's, Mary's, Joseph's, and John's. And all of us will want to hear every detail of it. I believe each one of us is that special to Him.

11

What About Tori, Ariel, and Jase?

IN THE STORIES of Peter and the other apostles, we observed how God took ordinary people and turned them into persons of great value. I think Paul's story demonstrates it best. But what about Tori Stafford and Ariel Yoder? Have you ever heard of them? Were these two children of less value to God?

Tori was a young nine-year-old Canadian girl who was abducted from her school, raped, tortured, and murdered by two psychopathic adults. On July 21, 2009, police confirmed that remains found were those of Tori. Her body was naked from the waist down, wearing only a Hannah Montana T-shirt and a pair of butterfly earrings that she had borrowed from her mother. Her lower half was significantly decomposed, and during an autopsy, it was determined that she had suffered a beating which caused lacerations to her liver and broken ribs. Her death was the result of repeated blows to the head with a claw hammer after being thrown alive into a large trash bag for execution. The disappearance and the subsequent investigation received massive media coverage across Canada. But 100 years from now, the odds are small that people will remember her name or her story. The question arises: Didn't God find value in her life?

Now, consider the life of Ariel Yoder. Ariel was six months old when she was diagnosed with spinal muscular atrophy (SMA.) She was given a life expectancy of one to two years and passed away at the age of 16 months. Spinal muscular atrophy (SMA) occurs when an individual has two copies of a mutated gene (one from each parent), causing them to develop a disorder that affects motor function. The chance of having this condition is approximately 1 in 10,000 live births, and about 1 of 50 people are carriers who have 1 copy of the mutated gene that could be passed down to their children.

Individuals with SMA do not produce enough survival motor neuron (SMN) protein. This is because they have a mutated or deleted survival motor neuron (SMN1) gene on both copies of the chromosome where the gene is located. SMN is crucial for the survival of motor nerve cells in the spinal cord, transmitting signals from the brain to the muscles. Without it, nerve cells die, muscles deteriorate, and children either never gain, or lose their ability to sit, stand, walk, and eventually swallow or breathe. Ariel was one of the "unlucky" ones, the 1 in 10,000 who received defective genes from her parents, leading to her death.

Like many others, both Tori and Ariel seemed to have died before having a chance to fulfill their God-given potential. Consequently, due to these tragedies and countless others, it's not surprising that many have lost faith in a God who allows such horrific events to occur every day. The woes of this world are not distributed equally, and after the death of their daughter, the Yoders learned that their next son, Jase, had also inherited the unfortunate genetic lottery.

In our fallen world, the list of sorrows seems almost endless. However, Tori's, Ariel's, and Jase's stories are not yet finished. One day, we will discover that they were as valuable to Him as Peter, Paul, and Mary. Just because we haven't seen the end from the beginning, as He has, it doesn't mean that God doesn't have tremendous plans for them and the millions of others who died in similar circumstances.

After their resurrection and restoration to their families and friends, having been made complete in our Lord's image and likeness, Tori could potentially be used by God in the restoration process of her two former enemies—the two people who took her life. While uncertain, it would not surprise me. Tori's name means the conqueror, the triumphant one, the victor! I believe millions will celebrate ecstatically with Tori and Ariel, as God destroys our last common enemy—death.

Ariel's name means "Lion of God," and was the name of the Archangel of healing and new beginnings! Jase means "healer, and the Lord is my salvation." All three of them will be well-known eternally because of God's love for them. They will serve as perfect examples of unmerited favor granted by a Savior who loved them and gave His life for them just as He did for all of His children. Yes, they are extremely valuable to Him and to all His family. Just look again at the names God gave them!

We are uncertain about which of harvests these three will be a part of, but what we do know is that after the third harvest, grace and peace— unconditional love—will stand in contrast to the old order, where men inflicted harm and caused death for selfish gain (John 16:1-4), and where random acts of nature loomed over us like the sword of Damocles, resulting in significant suffering and the onset of debilitating diseases, such as SMA. However, with His training on how to love Him and our neighbors as ourself, He will complete us and lift us up into another dimension, one where entropy, randomness, and luck no longer have roles to play – "Behold, I make all things new" (Rev. 21:5, KJV).

About a year after learning about Ariel and Jase, and after writing the above about them, we discovered my one-year-old granddaughter, Olivia, was also diagnosed with SMA. As you can imagine, the news was difficult to absorb. Nonetheless, I believe the Lord graciously allowed me to know, through the stories of Ariel and Jase, that He is in control. I believe that one day, Olivia will walk hand-in-hand with our Lord, the One who loves her, and the One who will give her life meaning and fill it full of joy.

Olivia's name originates from Latin, signifying "olive tree." In Psalms 52:8, she is likened to someone who regards themselves as a green olive tree in the House of God. This verse emphasizes that such individuals place their trust in the mercy and strength of God, rather than relying on their own strength. It is such a fitting description for this special little girl. I am confident that the Lord will bring healing to her, whether in this life, or the next, the timing will be perfect. I place my trust in His plans for her.

With this knowledge, 1 Corinthians 1:30 becomes rich in meaning: "It is because of Him that you are in Christ Jesus, who has become for us wisdom from God: our righteousness (dikaios – Justifier – the One who can fix us because He has the wisdom), holiness (our purifier), and redemption" (because He is our near kinsman redeemer) – NIV. The beautiful aspect of our learning process is what emerges from it – the third heaven, where God becomes "all in all." I pray that capturing a glimpse of it will transform your hope into trust, bringing along peace and comfort. This encapsulates Paul's gospel of "grace and peace." May our hearts and minds find rest in it.

Jesus: "For which of you, desiring to build a tower, does not first sit down and count the cost, whether he has enough to complete it? Otherwise, when he has laid down a foundation, and is not able finish, all who see it begin to mock him, saying, 'This man began to build, and was not able to finish'" (Luke 14: 28-30, RSV).

The Creator carefully assessed the cost, confident that He could fulfill His initial purpose – creating us in His image and likeness. On the Cross, the spikes in His hands and feet served as the finishing nails when He declared, "It is finished" (John 19:30, KJV). These words were documented for our benefit, providing sustenance to our faith as we navigate through life. In the same vein, we should uplift others with the perspective of the three heavens and the ineffable truths that can now be shared – the "good news of great joy, which will come to all people" (Luke 2:10, RSV).

The good news is emphasized in Matthew 1:17, where the genealogy of Jesus is succinctly summarized: "So, there were fourteen generations from Abraham to David, fourteen generations from David to the deportation to Babylon, and fourteen generations from the deportation to Babylon to Christ" (RSV). From the promises made to Abraham, stating that through his seed all families, nations, and lineages on earth would be blessed (Genesis 12:3, 18:18, and Acts 3:25), to the realization of those promises in Jesus, three distinct groups of people emerge.

Each group shares the same enumeration and is equally characterized by various sins. The assigned number for each group, fourteen, holds significance in the Bible, symbolizing salvation and rescue – deliverance. This represents God's promise to all three groups, treating them equally. Perhaps this is why He declares impartiality, showing no favoritism and being no respecter of persons. It seems like God is offering the same promise of perfection in Him to all three groups. Like Job's three daughters, they will be beautiful in their unique ways.

We often assess superiority based on outward appearances, deeming one group better than another. For instance, we might consider the second group superior to the third, and the first group the best of all. However, God's love is impartial, and as Paul asserted, there is no room for boasting. This notion is further underscored in Charles Spurgeon's analysis of the three individuals resurrected by Jesus. A summary of his sermon, describing our current condition and the imperative for our resurrection, is provided below. The complete sermon can be accessed online at: spurgeon.org/resource-library/sermons/spiritual-resurrection/#flipbook/

Spurgeon: "I shall begin by noticing, then, first of all, the condition of men by nature. **Men by nature are all dead** (emphasis mine)." He then describes Jairus's daughter, who had just passed. "She seems as if she were alive; her mother has scarce ceased to kiss her brow, her hand is still in her father's loving grasp, and he can scarcely think that she is dead; but dead she is, as thoroughly dead as she ever can be."

Next comes the case of the young man. Being dead longer, he has begun to be corrupt, and the signs of decay are upon his face, as they carry him to his tomb. Yet, though there were more manifestations of death on him, the little girl was just as dead as him, because "death really knows of no degrees."

The third case goes even further in its manifestation of death, where Martha, speaking to Jesus says, "Lord, by this time he stinketh; for he hath been dead four days." Spurgeon: "And yet, mark you, the daughter of Jairus was as dead as Lazarus; though the manifestation of death was not so complete in her case. All were dead alike."

Spurgeon then describes how all were quickened by Jesus in a different manner. The first was done privately, and the second publicly. Spurgeon: "It was done in the very street of the city. The maiden's life was given gently by a touch; but in the young man's case... by the touching of the bier... after that there comes the strong out-spoken voice—'Young man, I say unto thee, arise!'"

In the third case of Lazarus, "Jesus cried with a loud voice, Lazarus, come forth!" Spurgeon: "It is not written that he cried with the loud voice to either of the others. He spake to them; it was his word that saved all of them; but in the case of Lazarus, he cried to him in a loud voice..."

I trust you can discern the connection between these three stories and the three groups slated for resurrection. Furthermore, I hope to convey that despite their apparent differences, all three shared a commonality—they were all dead and in need of new life. In his complete sermon, Spurgeon points out that while one might seem more favorable than the others, at least from a human perspective, the fundamental reality remains unchanged—they are all the same, all in a state of death.

If there is still some uncertainty regarding the representation of these three individuals for the three groups to be revived, I will apply a bit of math to a previously discussed point, aiming to persuade you. Recall that the twelve-year-old girl was resurrected shortly after her death; the young man was brought back to life during his funeral procession just before being placed in the tomb, and Lazarus was already in the tomb after being dead for four days.

Now, let us apply some simple math. This time, I will make one assumption before converting days on the calendar of Moses to God's timetable as we did previously. Recall that a day on God's timetable is considered $1/50^{th}$ of a day on the calendar of Moses. Here is the assumption: Since we are all born into sin and death, I will presume that all three individuals whom Jesus raised were in a state of death from the very beginning—the first day of the calendar year, **and just as Spurgeon mentioned in the first two sentences of his sermon.** Now, let us proceed with the mathematical analysis.

If the first harvest/resurrection celebration began on the 14th day of Nissan (on Friday, 14 days after the beginning of the year) during the celebration at Passover, then, on God's timetable, the little girl, who I believe represented the first group, had only been dead less than 7 hours before she was resurrected. ($1/50^{th}$ of 14 days on Moses' calendar equals .28 of a day on God's timetable, or about 6.7 hours.)

If the second harvest celebration of the wheat began 49 days after the wave sheaf offering, occurring on the Sunday after the first day of Passover, then, according to the calendar of Moses, the young man, had only been dead a little more than a day before he was resurrected on God's timetable. ($1/50^{th}$ of 65 days (14+2+49) equals 1.3 days.)

If the third harvest celebration of grapes occurred 125 days later, per the calendar of Moses, then that group was in their 4th day of death on God's timetable when they are resurrected. (1/50th of 190 days (65+125) equals 3.8 days.)

Being dead for less than 7 hours clarifies why the little girl's funeral had not commenced. According to Hebrew tradition, the deceased were typically buried the following day after their death. This also explains why the young man was already in a coffin and being conveyed to his burial site when Jesus arrived on the scene. Lastly, it accounts for why Lazarus was already in the tomb, and as Martha described, had already started to emit an odor, having passed away 4 days prior.

When Jesus calls out to those in the three groups, they will be "made alive," just as illustrated in the three cases presented here and similarly to Saul's experience on the road to Damascus. I contend that each of these instances serves as a foreshadowing of three future resurrection events.

Remarkably, even those in the third group—His former enemies—can experience restoration after being immersed in death within a body of water, referred to as a lake. In this process, they are subjected to the fire of His unquenchable love, subsequently receiving life upon hearing His voice and emerging from the same body of water.

I propose that this is the moment when the water is transformed into wine during the third feast day celebration. This water now takes on the qualities of wine, symbolizing His blood shed for the remission of sin and flowing abundantly through the land of His enemies, outside the city, in outer darkness. Those who rise from their state of death emerge from that lake with their robes drenched/washed in the water/wine/blood of the Lamb. This is the richness of His kindness that will far exceed our expectations! This is who He is, the One that takes away the sin of the world."

Moreover, I believe this is the juncture when all will exclaim that God has "saved His best work for the last!" He will have accomplished what people deemed impossible—raising individuals from the second death. For mercy will triumph on the third day, because nothing is impossible for God. All those who are raised will recognize Him as the author and finisher of their faith, and this will serve as the answer to the question He poses to each of us: "Who do you say I am?"

At present, whether we are cognizant of it or not, God is weaving a story—His story—in us. He is intricately involved in every moment of our day. In his book, "The Healing Path," Dr. Dan Allender explains how God orchestrates and narrates our story. "Faith increases to the degree that we are caught up, enthralled by, and participating in His story in ours." He reminds us that approximately 70% of the Bible is written in narrative form.

Allender says, "God is a story-teller who weaves His presence into every story in the Bible. And how does He tell a story? With drama. He tells stories that excite, confuse, entice, disrupt, and change the human heart. Drama involves a beginning, with a setting, characters, and a search or problem to be solved, then, a middle with a plot that has moments of tragedy that brings a rise in tension and risk that demands faith, then an ending that instills confidence and invigorates hope." This is the "telos," denoting the goal toward which a story is being directed, the principal end, aim, or purpose.

Understanding His story interwoven with ours empowers us to confidently confront any life challenge, regardless of its difficulty, as we anticipate what lies beyond this moment. His goodness and overwhelming intelligence serve as the forces propelling an outcome that can only be described as miraculous. The Father's desire to mold His children in His image and likeness stems from pure love. I believe no one has fully grasped His heart, and comprehending His intellectual brilliance is beyond anyone's reach. In my story, I referred to His goodness and brilliance as "The Brightness Around Him."

As the Father of all (Matthew 23:9 & Ephesians 4:6), He is the perfect parent, understanding the thoughts of His children and foreseeing our every move since He intricately created us. Dr. Thomas Talbott employs an analogy likening our choices to playing a game of chess with the Grand Master. Despite the blessing of free will to make any move, the Grand Master will ultimately bring the novice to checkmate.

In John 12:32, Jesus declares, "And I, if I be lifted up from the earth, will draw all men unto Me" (KJV). The Greek word "draw" also encompasses the meaning "to drag," akin to a net. This is why a fish serves as a perfect symbol for Christianity, aligning with His statement about making His disciples "fishers of men."

Naturally, fish are not inclined to be caught, and similarly, our Freudian "ids" resist capture as well. Yet, He lures us into the net of His love, intricately woven into the fabric of grace. In the words of Thomas Talbott, His love—the net—is inescapable. When our hearts succumb to its capture, knees bow, tongues confess, willingly and thankfully, just as in the case for Paul, you, me, and others who will be resurrected from the second death.

12

The State of the Dead

CERTAINLY, VARIOUS QUESTIONS may come to mind as you explore the concept of three resurrections, especially if this is your first exposure to the idea. I acknowledge that numerous questions emerged for me as I began this journey. In the concluding chapters, my goal is to provide answers to some of these questions. Let us start with the initial query: How does the idea of three resurrections align with the belief that when Christians pass away, they immediately enter heaven?

The answer hinges on one's perspective. From the viewpoint of the person who has passed away, the most important one in the discussion, the concept of an immediate resurrection after death aligns well with the narrative we have presented thus far, and we will provide Biblical evidence for it in the upcoming discussion. However, for those still living, the notion that those who have preceded us in death are currently living another life in heaven, does not align within the framework of three resurrections, as I understand them.

From the study of physics, we learn that the measurement of time is not absolute; rather, it is relative to an observer's position and movement (speed). This is a law of physics established by God, and scientists have verified it with great accuracy. Consequently, where there is no movement, there is no time.

On multiple occasions, Jesus referred to death as "sleep," and as you may recall from our opening Corinthians text, Paul described those who died as "those who have fallen asleep." The metaphor of sleep appears at least nine times in the books of Matthew, Acts, Corinthians, and Thessalonians.

Consequently, the Bible often depicts the moment of resurrection as being "awakened" from sleep. Additionally, William Barclay informs us that the Greek word for cemetery means "a place where people sleep."

If death is comparable to sleep, then, from the perspective of the person who has passed away – the most significant individual in this conversation – their very next conscious moment after death is their resurrection! For them, no time has passed, similar to when you wake up from sleep without knowing how much time has elapsed. Hence, death is immediately succeeded by a resurrection.

However, this also implies that the deceased are not currently observing us from heaven. The deceased are at rest. The laws of motion further enlighten us that an object "at rest" and will remain "at rest" until acted upon by an outside force. This external force is the Spirit of Life promised by God on our resurrection day.

I understand how emotionally challenging this idea may be to some, because we desire our deceased loved ones to immediately be in a better place, and indeed they are! They are at rest, and thank God they are not looking down worrying about those of us who remain, or missing us as much as we miss them!

One hugely comforting thought for me is that after "closing our eyes" at death, we will immediately wake up with all our family and friends present, because we have been resurrected all at once, barring some of them being awakened in the first resurrection. We do not have to wait for anyone, unless they need further processing in the third group.

Question: If those who have passed away are presently living in heaven, does it imply that after the thousand-year reign, Michael will need to issue an order for everyone in heaven to return and enter their graves again, so that all in the tombs can be raised at the same hour? Will those enduring eternal torment in the lake of fire need to temporarily come out for judgment—only to be sentenced to hell once again?

The prevailing confusion, propagated by the belief that the dead are not truly dead, traces its roots back to the serpent's lie in the garden: "You shall not surely die," despite God's earlier declaration that "thou shalt surely die." The deceiver proclaimed man's soul to be immortal, but the terms "immortal soul" or "never-dying soul," cannot be found anywhere in the scriptures. What we do find are verses like: "The **soul** that sinneth, **it shall** die" (Ezekiel 18:20, KJV), and "for that which befalleth the sons of men befalleth beasts; even one thing befalleth them; as the one dieth, so dieth the other" (Ecclesiastes 3:19, KJV).

We also find other scriptures throughout the Bible that use these phrases concerning the state of the dead: "they do not know anything; they have no remembrance; they have no knowledge; they have no wisdom; they have no activity; they do not praise the Lord God, and their thoughts perish," because "the wages of sin is death."

As God told Hezekiah: "Set thy house in order: for thou shalt die, and not live" (II Kings 20:1, KJV). Why would God add that last phrase? Maybe He anticipated some being deceived, and He desired to let them know that death is the opposite of life, not another form of living. Furthermore, 1 Timothy 6:16 gives us another strong statement concerning humanity's present condition as mortal beings with this very clear declaration: "the King of kings, and the Lord of lords, who only (alone) hath immortality" (KJV).

Additionally, the confusion continues with the idea that we have a soul, when in fact, we are a soul. Genesis 2:7 (KJV) – "And the Lord formed man out of the dust of the ground, and breathed into his nostrils, the breath (spirit) of life, and man **became** a living soul." The Hebrew word for soul is "nephesh," and the Bible applies the term equally for man and animals in multiple scriptures. Both live and die.

We also learn more about the state of death from Deuteronomy 31:16 (KJV) – "And the Lord God said unto Moses, thou shalt sleep with thy fathers." The phrase, "sleep with thy fathers," is used 37 times in the books of Kings and Chronicles alone. The word, "sleep," is also used in connection with death in many other books including Job, Psalms, Daniel, Matthew, Mark, Luke, John, Corinthians, and Thessalonians.

But what about 1 Peter 4:6, where it seems to suggest that Jesus preached the gospel to the dead? A closer examination will reveal that the Gospel was proclaimed to those who are already deceased. Individuals from the past, such as Job, David, Isaiah, and Daniel, all believed and foretold a coming resurrection when all humanity would be judged in righteousness.

Additionally, 1 Peter 3:18-20 does not state that Christ went and delivered a sermon to deceased individuals. First, the phrase "went and" is not present in the original Greek but was later added by translators. Second, the word translated as "preached" means "to proclaim as a herald," distinct from preaching in the context of a revival, for which a different Greek word is used. Third, the proclamation was directed to spirits in prison, not the souls of men. These spirits are likely the same ones mentioned in Jude 6 and 2 Peter 2:4-5. Therefore, it was during Christ's resurrection that he proclaimed or heralded something—something likely good—to the spirits imprisoned in Tartarus, who had been disobedient in the days of Noah.

Concerning Luke 23:43, employing the original Greek words and a literal translation, Jesus told the thief on the Cross: "To you, I am saying today, with me, you will be in the paradise." The language may seem a bit awkward to us, but the phrase "to you, I am saying today" was a Hebrew idiom, emphasizing something noteworthy. This interpretation is supported by Rotherham's Emphasized Bible, the Concordant Literal New Testament, and the Companion Bible. Rotherham's translation is as follows: "And he said unto him, 'Verily I say unto thee this day: With me shalt thou be in paradise.'" **Furthermore, considering that Jesus was in the grave for three days, it is evident that He could not have been in paradise on the same day that He died.**

Moreover, the narrative of the rich man and Lazarus was a parable, the presence of Moses and Elijah on the mount was a vision, and the witch did not resurrect Samuel from the dead; Saul only "perceived" it was Samuel, as he was actually communicating with an evil "familiar spirit." If a witch could truly resurrect someone from the dead, it would present an entirely new problem. Additionally, Paul did not state, "to be absent from the body is to be present with the Lord," but rather, we would rather be away from the body AND at home with the Lord.

Recently, I discovered that some interpret the conversation Jesus had with the Sadducees, documented in the 22nd chapter of Matthew, as evidence that when God's people die, they immediately go to heaven. The Sadducees, distinct from the Pharisees, were a sect of religious elites who did not adhere to the belief in life after death, **hence denying resurrection.** Additionally, they held the conviction that the first five books of the Bible were the only scriptures to be accepted.

According to William Barclay, the Pharisees attempted to persuade the Sadducees of a resurrection from the dead using somewhat unconvincing arguments from Deuteronomy 31:16, 32:39, and Numbers 18:28. They also referenced Isaiah 26:19, stating "your dead shall live," but since this book was outside the books of the law, the Sadducees remained unconvinced.

In their effort to challenge the idea of resurrection, the Sadducees posed a seemingly absurd scenario to Jesus. They asked which husband would take a woman to be his wife in the resurrection if she had legally married seven times during her life on earth. Jesus addressed two errors in their questioning. First, they should not conceptualize heaven in terms of earth, as people in heaven will neither marry nor be given in marriage; they will be like angels. Second, He employed a common phrase found in the first five books of the Bible, "I am the God of Abraham, Isaac, and Jacob," to dismantle their skepticism regarding life after death. (I interpret Jesus as referring to the three groups destined for resurrection, as discussed in chapter 8.) Through this statement, Jesus offered evidence of the imperative need for a resurrection, emphasizing that God is the God of the living, not the dead (Matthew 22:32). His Son came to provide life, and life more abundantly – that is His essence!

To assert that this statement proves Abraham, Isaac, and Jacob are alive at this moment misses the point Jesus is making to the Sadducees. The emphasis is on the existence of life after death, and God, in His faithfulness, will bestow it, **just as He fulfilled His promises to Abraham, Isaac, and Jacob.** He has promised to eradicate death by granting life.

Furthermore, if Abraham, Isaac, Jacob, John the Baptist, Stephen, and numerous others were already alive in heaven when Paul wrote to the Corinthians, then Paul's assertions about all men in Christ being made alive in a future resurrection would have been a clear mistake. Moreover, Jesus would no longer hold the title "the beginning, the firstborn from the dead," as stated in Colossians 1:18 and reiterated in Revelation 1:5. He would also cease to be "the One who only (alone) has immortality."

Lastly, some assert that Jesus cleared out all who were in Hades during His three days in the tomb. If this were the case, then the description of those in this group would not align with the characteristics of those involved in the "first resurrection," as discussed in Revelation 20:4-6.

This brings us to "out-of-body experiences." Let me state upfront that I believe there are some remarkable experiences preceding death, along with dreams and visions of loved ones in heaven. I believe these can be granted by our Heavenly Father as encouragement to those left behind.

However, the data on out-of-body experiences (OBEs) and near-death experiences (NDEs) is inconsistent and does not align with the narrative purported by some Christians, who claim believers go to heaven immediately after death, while non-believers go to hell. The reality is that most people who lose their vital signs and come back to life never report anything about an out-of-body experience. The small number who do, perhaps 5% at best, include individuals from all religions, as well as atheists and agnostics. They commonly describe going to a place of happiness before returning to their physical bodies.

Additionally, experts have linked various medical and mental health conditions to out-of-body experiences (OBEs), including epilepsy, migraines, cardiac arrest, brain injuries, depression, anxiety, and Guillain-Barré syndrome, according to Healthline Media. They also provide the following information:

> "Dissociative disorders, particularly depersonalization-derealization disorder, can involve frequent feelings or episodes where you seem to be observing yourself from outside your body . . . Sleep paralysis, a temporary state of waking paralysis that occurs during REM sleep and often involves hallucinations, has also been noted as a possible cause of OBEs . . . Some people report having an OBE while under the influence of anesthesia . . . Other substances, including marijuana, ketamine, or hallucinogenic drugs, such as LSD, can also be a factor . . ."

In conclusion, science is uncertain about the reasons behind these out-of-body experiences (OBEs); they have some theories, but lack certainty. Nevertheless, God knows, and at this point, what Christians understand is that we can place our trust in His Word and express gratitude for His love and the hope He provides through the promise of immortality – a gift bestowed in one of the three resurrections. In the meantime, if God has granted you an OBE or NDE, consider yourself blessed, and thank you for shedding light on what awaits us when we transition from death to life.

Please note that this answer regarding the state of the dead was not intended to be an exhaustive analysis but rather to highlight a few aspects of the hope we have in Jesus. For a more in-depth exploration of this subject, I recommend Dr. Bullinger's writings; he was one of Oxford's leading scholars. Additionally, there are many other excellent works on the topic. For example, James Hollandsworth did a masterful job addressing the state of the dead in the fifth chapter of his book, the one we previously mentioned, "The Savior of All Men."

13

But What About? (FAQ's)

IN THIS FINAL chapter, I will address a few more questions that the reader may have while considering the ideas presented thus far. For example, what about Mark 9:43-46 – is it better to cut off body parts and enter into life maimed than go to hell?

As sleep was used by Jesus as a metaphor for death, there were many other instances where Jesus employed symbolic language to teach, prompting His audience to think. However, just like us, His listeners did not always catch on initially, and some of the fog remains to this day.

To gain the best understanding of any scripture, we need to grasp the context in which it was written. In this instance, Jesus held a private meeting with His disciples to address some of their misguided thoughts. He initiated the conversation by asking them, "What was it that you disputed among yourselves by the way?" In embarrassment, the disciples did not answer, but Jesus knew exactly what they had been arguing about: Who would be the greatest in the kingdom? He provided an answer, but it did not align with their thoughts. He told them that the greatest would be the last and the servant of all – the one who welcomed and received the least among them.

Jesus taught this with such gentleness and kindness, even using a child to drive home His point. He concluded the lesson by instructing them not to forbid those who were doing the work of the kingdom. The disciples had just rebuked a man because he was not in their inner circle. I believe the disciples got the message. This teaching method grants us the privilege of listening, as if we were there, looking over the shoulders of these men of Israel – Israel, the focal point of our Lord's ministry. And this is one of the most crucial points in this answer, for when reading the Gospels, we must remember who Jesus came to minister to first – Israel.

Sometimes, the things Jesus said were meant strictly for Israel, and they can only be applied to them in their circumstances. For example, He gave the covenant of the law to them, and no other nation. When He spoke concerning it, it was meant specifically for them, but we can still learn from their experiences. He knew we would be listening, so He included some lessons and admonition for us as well.

Continuing in this passage from Mark, observe how this approach will transform some seemingly outrageous statements into rational thought. Witness how this lesson becomes a very practical warning to Israel concerning their immediate future. This language was not meant to encourage an apotemnophilia disorder, nor was it intended to be some far-off warning into the future for the rest of the world designed to scare people everywhere. No, this warning was real, immediate, and its dire effects were about to swiftly descend upon Israel. Let us read on and see how this unfolds.

> Mark 9: 45-48: "And if thy foot offend thee, cut it off: it is better for thee to enter into life maimed, than to having two feet to be cast into hell . . . And if thine eye offend thee, pluck it out: it is better for thee to enter the kingdom of God with one eye, than to having two eyes to be cast into hell fire, where the worm dieth not, and the fire is not quenched" (KJV).

Taken at face value, these startling statements seem to insinuate that if you are maimed before entering God's kingdom, you will remain in the same condition after entering. Jesus also appears to be referring to immortal worms and the holy grail in physics – a source of perpetual energy! (I do not mean to take these statements lightly. His message was serious and a stern warning to Israel, and we can learn from it).

In this lesson, three body parts were used – hands, feet, and eyes. Notice there are two of each, and Jesus tells these Israelites to cut off, pluck out, or remove the one that offends. Most modern Bibles translate "offend thee" as "causes them to sin." Both phrases come from one Hebrew word, and neither phrase really conveys what we need to know.

The Hebrew term for "causes," as well as the Hebrew for "sin," are not found here. The Greek word used here is "skandalizo." It is derived from "skandalon," which was the name for a part of a trap or a snare to which bait is attached. Figuratively, it was a source of displeasure, a stumbling block, or an occasion to fall. So, according to Strong's Concordance, skandalizo means to put a stumbling block or impediment in the way, upon which another may trip and fall.

With this new set of lenses, our first question should be: "What was the snare or trap causing Israel discomfort? What was this stumbling block that would cause them to fall? Before we answer these questions, please notice that Jesus did not say to remove both hands, feet, and eyes, only the one that was causing them to stumble.

Which hand was holding the bait in a trap? Which foot was ensnared in that trap? Which eye was looking at this stumbling block as something to be desired? It sounds like these Israelites must have been facing a choice between two opposing ideas. One would be desired, but it would also entrap them, cause them to stumble, and lead to their fall. The other, which may have seemed less desirable at the time, would keep them from becoming entrapped, prevent them from falling, and keep them standing upright. Whatever choice they had to make would either allow them to live, or spell their doom.

The worms and the fire here are a reference to Jerusalem's garbage dump, the valley of Gehenna. This is a place where the worms feasted on the refuse, and the fire burned the trash continually, at least until it was consumed. That dump no longer exists, those worms are gone, and the physical fire no longer burns. I believe these Israelite boys and girls understood these references, because they lived there, but we have a more difficult time understanding, because we did not.

I also believe this lesson was about two covenants and the choice Israel was facing at that point in their history. As we have discussed previously at length, at that time Israel was under the covenant of the law, which brought the knowledge of sin (Romans 7:7-8) and the power of sin (1 Corinthians 15:56). The law produced wrath (Romans 4:15). It was the law that was causing Israel to stumble, because they could not keep it. For that reason, that covenant was faulty (Hebrews 8:7), and there was a need to replace it with something better (Galatians 2:16).

As we learned, Jesus knew that no flesh would be justified by the law (Romans 3:20), and He came to replace it with a new covenant of grace. He was bringing an end to the old order (Romans 10:4) and offering them a way out of their entanglement. The Jews should have understood this because when there is nothing standing between us and the law, death is the result. We need the mercy seat – Jesus – to cover the law on our behalf.

However, with few exceptions, the Jews would hold on to the law and reject God's grace. This choice would cause them to fall, bringing about the total destruction of their Temple and the demise of their nation in 70 A.D. They would be consumed like the trash in the garbage dump of Gehenna. This is an historical fact, and Jesus was warning them about it. If they remained under the law, they would be judged by it. With Israel, the Lord painted a picture of what happens when we reject His grace. This theme is summed up in the words of Paul:

> Romans 9:31-10:4: "but that Israel who pursued the righteousness which is based on the law did not succeed in fulfilling that law. Why? Because they did not pursue it through faith, but as if it were based on works. They have **stumbled** over the **stumbling stone**, as it is written, 'Behold, I am laying in Zion a stone that **will make men stumble**, a rock that **will make them fall** (skandalon); and he who believes in Him will not be put to shame.' Brethren, my heart's desire and prayer to God for them is that they may be saved. I bear them witness that they have a zeal for God, but it is not enlightened. For, being ignorant of the righteousness that comes from God, and seeking to establish their own, they did not submit to God's righteousness. For Christ is the end of the law, that every one who has faith may be justified" (RSV).

Because Israel mistakenly believed it was within their ability to keep the law, they clung to the old covenant and faced its curses. Consequently, God would temporarily bury them in "hades," the grave, the land of the unseen. It would be a challenging lesson for Israel to learn, and later, even the Gentiles would find grace difficult to accept. For Israel, relinquishing the old covenant would be like cutting off a limb or plucking out an eye; they believed they would be maimed without it. Similarly, for the Gentiles, as with Israel, embracing grace is a formidable challenge to our egos, as our tendency is to rely on ourselves rather than on the righteousness of God.

For those of us who were never under that law covenant, observing Israel's reaction reflects who we are. The lesson for all of us is that self-righteousness and self-reliance will not lead anyone to the promised land. This was the same decision Adam and Eve faced in the garden – choosing between eating from the tree of life (the covenant of grace) or the tree of the knowledge of good and evil (the covenant of the law). Opting for the latter resulted in death for Adam, Eve, and Israel.

Fortunately, that is not the end of the story. Jesus once relayed a parable about a treasure buried in a field. Israel was His treasure, and even though He buried them as a nation in 70 A.D., He still planned to resurrect them at some point in the future. The field (the world) is His and all that is in it. He paid for it, including the treasure He buried in that field.

As we learned previously, there is coming a day "when all Israel shall be saved" (Romans 11:26). In order to accomplish that task, God's plan called for another type of worm – Jesus – to give His life, so that life could be given to Israel once again. His plan also called for another type of fire, the fire of His love, which will purge Israel and make them complete in His image and likeness.

Hints of this promise of good news for Israel are found in our text, where Jesus declares that "all will be salted with fire." He emphasizes that "salt is good." Indeed, His plan, His generosity, is not just good but exceeds our imagination! "For every one will be salted with fire, and every sacrifice shall be salted with salt. Salt is good, but if the salt has lost its saltiness, wherewith will ye season it? Have salt in yourselves, and have peace with each other" (Mark 9:49-50, KJV).

In the second chapter of Leviticus, we find instructions concerning the cereal offering – the offering of grain. In it, oil (God's anointing) was to be poured over the grain, but no honey or leaven was to be added. However, salt was to be poured out on the grain. Then, to drive home the point, the mixture was burnt on an altar of fire. This salting with fire would make "a sweet savor (odor) unto the Lord."

Why was honey or leaven not to be used? Concerning honey, nothing needed to be added to this sacrifice to make it any sweeter than it already would be to our God. No self-righteousness, no self-reliance, no work done by us needs to be added to His work on the Cross. Regarding leaven, He once warned to "beware the leaven of the Pharisees." Why did Jesus single out the leaven of the Pharisees? The answer is that this leaven represented what the Pharisees taught – that entrance into God's Kingdom would be based on a man's ability to fulfill the Law, relying on his own righteousness (similar to the mindset of Nicodemus and reflective of the mindset of Israel).

Independence and self-reliance are valuable qualities. Just as leaven causes bread to rise, these traits can elevate a person in everyday life. However, they are insufficient for our salvation. Our efforts and righteousness will inevitably fall short, as demonstrated by the example our Father left throughout history – Israel. The good news is that He is willing to bestow His righteousness upon us on our behalf.

Returning to our passage in Mark, and in conclusion, Jesus conveys the notion that it is beneficial when His fire purges us of our self-righteousness and the belief that we are superior to others. Through this process, we can become better servants to all, acquiring the ability to live in peace and harmony with our brothers and sisters. This aspect is applicable to all of us, not solely to the Israelites in that specific context.

Let us not return to the position where Israel once stood under the old law covenant. Instead, let us move forward with our feet planted on the path of His grace, our eyes focused on that grace, and our hands holding onto His grace. This is the only way we can live in peace with Him and each other in His kingdom.

Final reflections: Recall the events on the Mount of Transfiguration. Peter suggested building three tabernacles – one for Moses, Elijah, and Jesus. God intervened, instructing them to listen to His Son. Peter, James, and John promptly fell to the ground in fear until Jesus reassured them. **Upon rising, the Law and the Prophets were gone!** Only Jesus, the One who saves us by His grace, remained.

What about Matthew 7:13-14? "Enter by the narrow gate, for the gate is wide and the way is easy, that leads to destruction, and those who enter by it are many. For the gate is narrow and the way is hard that leads to life, and those who find it are few" (RSV).

In that era, it was customary to access a city through a broad road leading to a wide gate. However, smaller gates were also present along narrower paths, though rarely utilized. A. E. Knoch observed that these paths were infrequently taken, as the small gates were closed during the day and locked at night. Choosing the broad road was more convenient.

If this were the case, why would anyone choose the narrow path? It would not be the natural choice, and I believe this provides a significant clue on how to interpret our Lord's teaching here. Jesus was instructing his disciples and cautioning them about Israel's precarious situation and imminent downfall as a nation due to their failure to recognize Him as their Messiah. "Many" in Israel believed that adherence to the law could secure their salvation, both individually and as a nation. However, Israel's history had already demonstrated the frailty of human nature and the futility of achieving salvation through obedience to the law.

The covenant of grace would be God's response, and only "few" in Israel would embrace this new way. Given human nature, it was quite natural for Israel to choose the broad road—believing they could attain salvation through their own efforts. It would require a lesson in humility (the narrow path) to acknowledge failure. In 70 A.D., the destruction of the "many" unfolded just as Jesus had predicted in the Olivet Discourse (Matthew 24:34). This is an historical fact.

However, Jesus did not accept this outcome as the end of the matter. He would now take the way of the Cross as a ransom for the "many" (Matthew 20:28). This is the same "many" who entered the wide gate on the road of self-reliance, self-righteousness, and ultimately, destruction. The late Jan Bonda stated: "Jesus goes the way of the cross to open for these many the way of escape from punishment, ensuring that their 'going away to punishment' is followed by their return. For that reason, He became obedient until death on the cross."

What about Matthew 25:46? Here is another example of how Jesus used metaphoric language to warn Israel of God's coming judgment upon their generation in Matthew 25:46. "And these shall go away to punishment age-during, but the righteous to life age-during" from Young's Literal Translation, or "And these shall be coming away into chastening eonian, yet the just into life eonian" from the Concordant Literal Version. Note: The

King James Version incorrectly translated a portion of it with the phrases "everlasting punishment" and "life eternal."

What follows are just a few comments about this verse from Mike Owens' website that we referenced previously: *TheHellVerses.com.* Concerning this one, Mike summarized with:

- The word "punishment" comes from the Greek word "kolasis," which is better translated as "chastisement" since "kolasis" was not a word used for retribution but for discipline that was in the interest of setting things right. "Kolasis" was used for the pruning of trees to help them grow better.

- Matthew 25:46 is recorded as the close of a long day in Jesus' recorded ministry. The conversation began after Jesus left the temple where He criticized the religious leadership. In Matthew 23, we find some of the harshest language Jesus employed. This language was NOT aimed at the average citizen nor at the heathen nations surrounding Israel. It was, in fact, aimed at the Jewish leadership—the Pharisees, scribes, and lawyers.

- Within this portion of Matthew's writings, Jesus is making a very startling and irritating point: the religious and Jewish political leadership of His day was utterly corrupt. Judgment was at the door.

- Among Jesus' descriptive words for the Jewish leadership of His generation were "blind guides, hypocrites, den of snakes, sons of Gehenna (the local city dump translated Hell by some translations), white-washed tombs, and fools. After a thorough thrashing, Jesus declared to them, "I send you prophets, wise men, and scribes: some of them you will kill and crucify, and some of them you will scourge in your synagogues and persecute from city to city, that on you may come all the righteous blood shed on the earth, from the blood of righteous Abel to the blood of Zechariah, son of Berechiah, whom you murdered between the temple and the altar. Assuredly, I say to you, all these things will come upon THIS generation" (not some generation one or two thousand years later) (Matthew 23:34-36, KJV).

- A careful reading of Josephus' "War of the Jews" reveals everything Jesus foretold in these verses was perfectly fulfilled within that very generation of Jews. Matthew 25:46 is a part of this warning to them, not a warning to anyone after 70 AD.

- Thayer describes "to go away" or "going off" with regards to Strong's, G565 ἀπέρχομαι, equivalent to "going away from" or "departing evils" unlike the common understanding of being thrown into a pit of fire. This verse closes Matthew's explanation of the separation of the goats and sheep. If we are to assume any one individual meets the qualifications of a sheep and another a goat, this becomes problematic considering most of us meet the requirements for both. A close look into these qualifications will reveal that most everyone we know qualifies as a sheep and a goat - simultaneously.

- Nowhere in Matthew's text are we told anything about believers or unbelievers. Matthew's use of rhetoric is frequent, and we see it here. Endless punishment in fire is no more literal than the fact that nations nor individuals are sheep or goats.

- Many sense their certainty of everlasting life from the second half of this verse and John 3:16. However, believers should not find their assurance of "eternal" life from the term "eternal" - especially in light of the fact that this term has been inaccurately translated here. Our assurance of endlessness in Glory comes from our inclusion or adoption into the lineage of the one who is everlasting, the Last Adam, Jesus Christ. (Romans 5:16-19 and 1 Corinthians 15:22) This accomplishment was brought on by His faithfulness, not ours.

Final Question: What about Lazarus and Dives? We will conclude the book with one more example of the use of metaphorical language in another parable concerning Lazarus and Dives. There is much to be said about this parable, and I believe it will be best to leave you with some highlights from Mike Owens' summary of it on his website.

"There was a certain rich man who was clothed in purple and fine linen and who lived in luxury every day. At his gate laid a beggar named Lazarus, covered with sores and longing to eat what fell from the rich man's table. Even the dogs came and licked his sores. The time came when the beggar died and the angels carried him to Abraham's side. The rich man also died and was buried. In hell (hades), where he was in torment, he looked up and saw Abraham far away with Lazarus at his side. So he called to him, 'Father Abraham, have pity on me and send Lazarus to dip the tip of his finger in water and cool my tongue, because I am in agony in this fire.' But Abraham replied, 'Son, remember that during your lifetime you your good things, and Lazarus received bad things, but now he is comforted here, and you are in agony. And besides all this, between us and you a great chasm has been fixed, so that those who want to go from here to you cannot, nor can anyone cross over from there to us.' He answered, 'Then I beg you, father, send Lazarus to my father's house, for I have five brothers. Let him warn them, so they don't also come to this place of torment.' Abraham replied, 'They have Moses and the Prophets; let them listen to them.' 'No, Father Abraham,' he said, 'but if someone from the dead goes to them, they will repent.' He said to him, 'If they do not listen to Moses and the Prophets, they will not be convinced even if someone rises from the dead'" (Luke 16:19-31, NIV).

- These two men, Lazarus and the rich man, represent two classes of people and illustrate how the self-righteous (Pharisees) viewed themselves and their disregard for the rest of the world. The Pharisees claimed exclusive access to God and His blessings, creating an atmosphere of exclusion, distinction, and judgmental attitudes in which Jesus tells this story.
- Abraham replied, "Son" (Abraham addresses the rich man as "Son," likely indicating that the "rich man" is a descendant of Abraham), "you remember that in your lifetime you received your good things – the law, the prophets, and the covenant." The rich man is undoubtedly symbolic of the Jews/Pharisees.
- In that day, Jews commonly referred to Gentiles as dogs. For example, in Matthew 15:26, Jesus initially refuses to help a Gentile woman, stating that it isn't right to throw the children's (Jew's) bread to the dogs (Gentiles). The woman responds that even the dogs eat the leftovers from their master's table.
- Many agree that this is the final parable in a chain of five given by Jesus, which begins at Luke 15:3. The four parables that immediately precede this one are:

- o A) The lost and found sheep
- o B) The lost and found coin
- o C) The lost and found "prodigal" son
- o D) The shrewd manager

Each of these parables addresses the subject of something or someone that is lost. The primary avowal of ownership and value is in the ability to be "lost." No one can be reckoned as lost unless they are owned. Worth is declared when something or someone is deemed to be lost and sought after.

- Martin Luther taught that the story was a parable about the rich and poor in this life, and the details of the afterlife should not be taken literally. Therefore, we conclude that the bosom of Abraham signifies nothing else than the Word of God (Church Postil 1522–23).
- These parables were addressed directly to the tax collectors and common "sinners" while the Pharisees were muttering comments and listening in.
- As we will see in the upcoming points to consider, this allegory is revealing something profound about the old covenant - the law - coupled with man's efforts and the contrast with the new covenant - Grace - based on our weakness and His mercy.
- Other facts about the rich man include that he had five brothers, feasted sumptuously, and was dressed in purple and fine linen. All of these details pointed to these Jews, the Pharisees. Judah had five brothers from his mother, Leah.
- Purple is symbolic of royalty, and it was the citizens of the southern Kingdom of Judah that returned from the Babylonian area to rebuild Jerusalem. They became known as "Jews," which technically speaking is short for "the people of Judah." The Pharisees knew their heritage well, and they surely knew Jesus was speaking about them when referring to the rich man.
- The name Lazarus is Greek for Eliezer or Eleazar. It is likely that this is Abraham's number one assistant, according to most interpretations. He is the unnamed slave, the elder of the household, who controlled all that was his in Genesis 24. Eliezer, or Lazarus,

of Damascus was Abraham's Syrian Gentile servant set to inherit Abraham's house if Abraham had no heir (Genesis 15:2).

- Many agree that the poor man was an image of the tax collectors and sinners who were looked down on by the elite Pharisees. Because the Pharisees considered riches to be a sign of God's blessings, it was quite natural for them to consider the poor as less important than themselves.

- The story has nothing to say about belief in Jesus as the Christ or even about faith in God. The story does not say the rich man was bad or evil, or that Lazarus was good or righteous.

- After identifying the symbols in a story like this, it's important to remember that a parable is a short allegorical story designed to illustrate or teach some truth, principle, or lesson. It is not to be taken literally.

- With regards to the denial by Abraham to allow the rich man to tell others, Richard Bauckham writes, "The means of revelation which the reader expects it to acquire as the story proceeds are denied it. The story in effect deprives itself of any claim to offer an apocalyptic glimpse of the secrets of the world beyond the grave. It cannot claim eyewitness authority as a literal description of the fate of the dead. It only has the status of a parable. It is part of a story told to make a point. The point is no more than the law and the prophets say – and that no more than the law and the prophets is required."

- Alfred Edersheim notes, "Is this teaching a simple reversal of situations in the next life? Does it mean that only the destitute and miserable get saved and the rich go to hell? Of course not! So let's consider these two figures. We see in vs. 24 that the rich man said, "Father Abraham." Likewise, we saw that Abraham acknowledges him as his "child" in vs. 25. This identifies him as a Jew, and this is the figure he plays in this parable. The rich man is a figure of the Jews (specifically, the Pharisees)."

- It is safe to say that this allegory is not about who is going to "heaven" or "hell." Nor is it about "eternal" destinies. If this were the case, then we'd have to redefine hades and the supposed qualifications for heaven or hell: those who are poor go to heaven and those who are rich go to hell.

- To assume "Abraham's bosom" is heaven is pure conjecture with no biblical or cultural support. While Abraham was used in a very unique and powerful way, he is a mere man born of Adam like us all.

- If "heaven" was a place where we could see "the lost" in a place of torment, then that would be a sad and miserable place. In fact, the concept of "hell" displaces any genuine joy in "heaven."

- David once said in his later years that in all of his days, he had never seen the righteous forsaken, nor even his seed begging for bread (Psalms 37:25). Why would Jesus use a man sick and full of sores begging at the gate as a representative of His followers?

- Abraham received many great promises. In his seed, all families, peoples, and nations would be blessed. Kings would also come from his loins, and the King of Kings, the Messiah, would come from his loins - and these promises were kept in Abraham's bosom. Also included in Abraham's bosom was knowledge learned by experience, that these promises were not the result of human effort, as seen in Abraham and Sarah's attempt to fulfill their desire for a child by using Hagar and not waiting.

- Paul, in Romans 7:6 and Galatians 2:19, makes two amazing statements that provide the breakthrough we need to understand the symbolic nature of the death of the poor man: "But now we have been released from the Law, having died to that by which we were bound, so that we serve in newness of the Spirit and not in oldness of the letter" (NKJV) and "For through the law I died to the law, that I might live to God" (NKJV).

- The death of the poor man in the parable had nothing to do with physical death. It was the Jews' death to the old covenant that Jesus was speaking about. As a result of accepting grace, they were carried by the Spirit into Abraham's bosom.

- The rich man's demise was a representation of what those who desired to stay under the law would experience. Dead in misery under the weight of an agreement they could not keep. They would be in anguish. Again, this has nothing to do with physical death.

- It was likely quite obvious to the Jews that this parable was painting a picture and telling them that the gateway to the kingdom is by God's mercy, not human righteousness or efforts, which they were quite proud of.

- The Great Gulf Fixed: This seems to be making it clear that the two covenants, law and grace, are polar opposites. They cannot be mixed. The law was conditional, while grace is entirely unconditional; otherwise, it is not grace. Yet, many in Christianity today try to present grace as something that is conditional, even if it's merely "acceptance" that triggers God's mercy - sometimes referred to as decisional regeneration.

- The story of Jacob and Esau is another allegory about the two covenants. When Jacob lost the struggle, all he could do was hold on and ask for blessings. At that moment, he realized he never needed to struggle to make the promises happen; all he had to do was trust God for them, and God would do the work. He entered the next phase of his life lame, being carried on God's shoulders to Abraham's bosom, and his name was changed to Israel, which means "God rules."

- How would you feel if you were under a contract that you could not keep? Wouldn't you be miserable? This is the place where Israel found itself, and Jesus came to get them out of that contract. In this parable, it is plain to see that mankind cannot get to grace, traverse the great gulf to be in grace, with human effort; they must be carried by the Spirit.

- The terms "torment" and "fire" or "heat" mentioned in verses 23 and 24 are interesting. "Torment" is a term used in metallurgy, specifically in Greek as "basanidzo," which referred to the testing of metals with the touchstone and figuratively meant to be tested or to experience a hard time.

- Abraham represents the place of God's acceptance, care, and comfort – and Paul looks to him as a figure of God's chosen who would produce the Promise (figured in Isaac), the Messiah, who would inaugurate the new covenant, from which the old arrangement (represented by the scribes and Pharisees) was to be excluded.

- Alfred Edersheim makes another excellent observation: In the fire of God's dealings, the once-rich man becomes aware of his need for the water of life and realizes that the outcasts have it. He asks for mercy. However, his condition and his time of judgment have placed a gulf between himself and those now being graced with God's favor (a gulf that only Christ can span). Yet, we can see another change happening in him: he begins to think of others. He wants

Lazarus to evangelize his brothers so that they will not have the same separation.

• Peter Hiett adds this perspective: Judah, the rich man, wasn't thirsty for the Messiah and thought he could pay for all his drinks. Hades makes a person thirsty for grace, and Jesus promises that he will give to the thirsty. He destroys the chasm: "Every valley shall be exalted, and the mountain and hills laid low." - Further noting: "To the thirsty, I will give from the spring of the water of life without payment" (Rev. 21:6, also 22:17, RSV).

• In the last verse, Abraham tells the rich man (representing the self-righteous Pharisees) that if they do not listen to Moses and the Prophets, they will not be convinced even if someone rises from the dead. Jesus could possibly be referring to: 1) The "rich man," 2) Lazarus (the brother of Mary and Martha), or 3) Himself, the Messiah. Either way, their hearts have proven to be stubborn, and seeing someone experience resurrection would not convince them. [It is interesting to remember the eight days of stubbornness declared by the disciple Thomas after the resurrection of Jesus, yet he believed once he saw the risen Christ – just as Jesus told Nicodemus how people would be healed (saved) when they saw the accursed one lifted up.]

• In the second parable, the lost coin is found, and the owner loses none. Mike Meeker noted there were ten coins. Could it be these represent the ten lost tribes of Israel who were taken into captivity by the Assyrians and scattered among the nations? Their lostness is only temporary, for the owner seeks them until he has them all in his possession (Deuteronomy 4:25-31).

• Here's what we might learn from these 5 parables: You can go your own way, and our Savior will not give up until all the lost sheep are found, all the lost coins are found, and all the lost family members return home safely. If one is looking for a summary of how the story ends for mankind; right upfront, Jesus ties it all together with a three-stranded cord that is a major part of this often-misunderstood parable, and all are directed at the Pharisees.

• This is the only place where "hades" (the grave; the realm of the dead – vs. 23) is associated with fire, and it is within what many view as a parable. A study of the figure of fire, as used in Scripture, will show that it signifies God - which brings purification – but that is a study all of its own. Malachi 3:1-6; 1 Cor. 3:9-17.

- John Lightfoot (1602–1675) considered the parable as a parody of the Pharisee belief concerning the Bosom of Abraham, and from the connection of Abraham saying the rich man's family would not believe even if the parable Lazarus was raised, to the priests' failure to believe in the resurrection of Christ: Anyone may see how Christ points at the infidelity of the Jews, even after that himself shall have risen again.

- The idea of penal torment falls apart with this parable. The "penalty" is that a person cannot "pay." People in stress, pain, and confusion are convinced that they must pay... they have not come to the end of themselves. When we come to the end of ourselves, we're thirsty - and it's grace that stares us in the face.

- The bottom line: With Israel's failure, God sent His Son to the rescue offering them a better covenant. However, the Jewish leadership wanted to hang on to the old. This is the backdrop to the parable about the poor man and the rich man.

Thank you, Mike, for this very informative summary and allowing me to share it. Condensing the input from all those contributors must have taken a lot of work. Myself and others really appreciate it.

At this point, I hope this book has provided enough information for you to consider "The Third Heaven, and the unutterable things that can now be told." At a minimum, I pray the contents will help us grasp a little more about the enormity of God's goodness and superior intelligence. I hope the byproduct will increase our affections for Him and our trust in His plans. The idea of a third resurrection, where His former enemies can be rescued from outer darkness and the second death, leaves us with much to think about. The implications are staggering, and I hope you will find a greater measure of peace and joy as you discuss them with our Heavenly Father.

APPENDIX

For an enlightening exercise, read the book of Matthew from start to finish in one sitting. Relax and read it as if you are encountering it for the first time. I believe you will be surprised to realize how many of our Lord's warnings were directed specifically at the religious leadership of Israel. For instance, when He mentioned "this generation," He was addressing them directly.

Dr. Ken Gentry, in his book "The Olivet Discourse Made Easy," provides a summary of what you might discover as you read Matthew. I will endeavor to summarize Ken's writings and include a few of my own observations.

- In the first chapter, Matthew intentionally begins with three groups of fourteen generations, each indicating a phase Israel has experienced, all pointing to the need for a Messiah—Jesus.
- In the second chapter, Matthew illustrates how Jerusalem would be the center of antagonism towards the Savior. There, we find that Herod was troubled by His birth, "and all Jerusalem with him." Later, the crowds in Jerusalem would choose a notorious prisoner to be released over Jesus. Also, when Pilate asked them what he should do with Jesus, "they all said, 'Let Him be crucified!'"
- Prior to the beginning of our Lord's ministry, Matthew 3:2 warned them to: "Repent, for the kingdom of heaven is at hand" (RSV). John the Baptist also warned in verse 10 that "the axe is already at the root of the trees" (RSV).
- In chapter 4, we find Jesus beginning His ministry but retreating to Galilee after hearing of John's imprisonment. This was another negative portrayal of the religious and political situation in Israel.

- Matthew 5-7 highlights Israel's negative condition again and the approaching doom. We are informed that many (in Israel) would enter the broad gate that leads to destruction.
- Matthew 8 opens with a call for repentance in Israel, or if not, they would be cast into outer darkness.
- Jesus teaches in Matthew 9 that His new covenant of grace could not be contained within the old Jewish system's covenant of the law.
- In Matthew 10, Jesus limits His personal ministry to Israel and provides them opportunities to repent.
- Dr. Gentry, regarding Matthew 11, states, "Jesus states 'this generation' is rejecting both his and John the Baptist's ministries." Jesus had declared John to be the fulfillment of Elijah's return, whose ministry was to prepare the nation for "the great and terrible day of the Lord."
- In Matthew 12: 39, 41, and 42 (KJV), Jesus calls Israel an "evil and adulterous generation" and refers to them as "this wicked generation," who "the men of Nineveh shall rise in judgment with this generation" along with the queen of the south who "shall rise up in the judgment with this generation and shall condemn it."
- In Matthew 13: 14-15 (NIV), Jesus says of Israel: "In them is fulfilled the prophecy of Isaiah: 'You will be ever hearing but never understanding; you will be ever seeing but never perceiving. For the people's heart has become calloused... Otherwise, they might see... hear... understand... and turn, and I would heal them." In 15:7, Jesus rebukes the Pharisees and scribes, calling them "hypocrites."
- Again, in chapter 16, Jesus calls the Pharisees and Sadducees "hypocrites" and "a wicked and adulterous generation." He also calls Israel an "unbelieving and perverse generation" in chapter 17.
- In Matthew 18 and Mark 9, Jesus speaks to Israel about their choice between staying with the old covenant, which was causing them to stumble, or choosing to accept their Messiah and the new covenant of Grace that was being offered to them.
- In Matthew 19, Jesus speaks of a time of regeneration when the old passes away, and the new age is inaugurated – the age of grace. Dr. Gentry, concerning Matthew 20, states: "In this chapter, we learn that Christ once again prophesies that the religious leaders of Israel

(including their chief priests) will condemn him to death... He is not painting a pretty picture of Israel's first-century spiritual condition and moral conduct."

- In Matthew 21, Jesus makes a dramatic entry into Jerusalem. Mark records the cursing of the fig tree and speaking about the mountain (Israel) being cast into the sea as occurring prior to Him going to the Temple to cleanse it. Evidently, God's House was not operating as He had designed, and therefore, Jesus acted out what scholars call "prophetic theater," per Dr. Gentry. With this cleansing, Jesus not only predicts the destruction of the Temple, but here he symbolically acts out the upcoming 70 A.D. scene.

- In Matthew 22, Jesus speaks a parable concerning the wedding of a king's son. The king is God, and Jesus is His son. The people who were invited to the wedding (Israel) refuse to come, and some of them murder the king's servants (the prophets). The king is enraged and sends an army, which destroys and burns their city. Obviously, this was all prophetic of what was to come for that generation.

- In Matthew 23, Jesus calls the scribes and Pharisees "hypocrites," "blind guides," "fools and blind," "children of them which killed the prophets," "serpents," "generation of vipers," like unto whited sepulchers, which indeed appear beautiful outward, but are within full of dead men's bones and of all uncleanness. He pronounces seven woes upon the Pharisees, emphatically stating that all these things shall come upon this generation. This statement is found again in Matthew 24, serving as the introduction to the Olivet Discourse.

- We should also note how Jesus is found weeping over Jerusalem at the end of chapter 23. Then, He declares their house would be left desolate, just as it happened in 70 A.D. Dr. Gentry says, "This brief survey of Matthew's gospel is important for the literary and historical context of the Olivet Discourse with its warning of Israel's judgment in 70 A.D. Both Jesus' repeated teaching and actions clearly highlight God's approaching wrath upon Israel. This understanding of Matthew is so clear as to be undeniable."

Thank you, Ken, for your amazing insights and allowing me to share them.

Without adopting a preterist, dispensationalist, futurist, or any other "ism's" point of view, I aim to highlight some facts about our Lord's predictions and His responses to His disciples' questions about when the Temple would be destroyed and what signs would accompany His coming in judgment upon Israel at the end of that age.

It has been well-documented by Jewish theologians and historians how "the generation before the destruction [of the temple] witnessed a remarkable outburst of Messianic emotionalism . . . to be attributed to . . . the prevalent belief induced by the popular chronology of the day that the age was on the threshold of the millennium" (Jewish theologian Abba Hillel Silver.) Josephus, Justin Martyr, and others like Hippolytus record "there arose some saying, I am Christ, as Simon Magus, and the rest whose names I have not time to reckon." This fulfilled Christ's prediction that many would come in His name proclaiming themselves to be the Christ.

The historical record is also clear about an unusual number of earthquakes and famines in the area occurring before the fall of Jerusalem. But the one prediction that is the most insightful to me is when Jesus warned about wars and rumors of wars with nations rising up against nations.

It is very clear from history that until the end of Nero's reign in 68 A.D., the Mediterranean world had been at peace for a long period. The "Age of Peace" had been established by Augustus in 17 B.C., and historians note that there were neither wars nor battles until the time of the Jewish rebellion. In 68-69 A.D., the turmoil quickly became so severe that the Roman Empire almost collapsed. Several nations revolted and tried to separate themselves from the Empire. According to historians, this turmoil came unexpectedly, and Jesus was the One who foretold it!

Jesus also predicted that the disciples would face persecution, hatred, and death. Additionally, He mentioned that the gospel of the kingdom would be preached in all the world. This statement posed a challenge for me until I came across Luke 2:1 and Acts 11:28, where I discovered that "the world" referred to the Roman world. Acts 2:5 provides evidence for this. It mentions "devout men from every nation under heaven" dwelling in Jerusalem during Peter's sermon. Moreover, in Colossians 1:6 & 23, Paul declares that the gospel "was preached to every creature which is under heaven" (KJV). Additionally, in Romans 10:18, Paul informs us that the sound of the gospel, preached by preachers, **"went to all the earth, and**

their words to the end of the world" (KJV). In Romans 1:8, Paul thanks God "for you all, that your faith is spoken throughout the whole world" (KJV).

Finally, some believe that Matthew 24:21, where it speaks about a great tribulation not seen since the beginning, nor ever shall be, proves He was not referring to 70 A.D. However, this view is taken totally out of context. The preceding verses inform us exactly when this occurred. Jesus told them, when you see the abomination of desolation spoken of through Daniel standing in the holy place, then, verse 16: "let those in Judea flee to the mountains" (NIV). Compare that language with the same account in Luke 21:20-21 (NIV), which warns that when they see Jerusalem surrounded by armies, then, "let those who are in Judea flee to the mountains."

This identifies the abomination and the holy place as the Roman army and Jerusalem respectively. As the capital of the Holy Land, Jerusalem was where the holy Temple resided. Jesus tells the Christians in all of Judea that when they see these things, flee! Matthew 24:20-21 (KJV): "But pray that your flight be not in the winter, neither on the Sabbath day. For (because) then shall be great tribulation, such as was not since the beginning..." According to Josephus and others, this is exactly what the Christian population in Israel did when they saw the Roman army surrounding Jerusalem. They fled to the mountains and escaped the terrible siege.

Just as Jesus had warned, in 70 A.D., God's wrath fell upon Jerusalem, and the Spirit left the old physical temple and came to temples not made with hands. According to various historians, including Josephus, the horrors and unspeakable events that occurred in and around Jerusalem from 67-70 A.D. match perfectly with the language and prophecies found in Isaiah 66 and in Jesus' warnings to the religious leadership of His day.

Matthew's words, informing us that there will never be a tribulation like this again, were meant for Israel, those who had been chosen to usher in God's Kingdom on earth. Let's read Ezekiel 5: 5-11. There we find God's prophecy on the destruction of Jerusalem and the reasons for it:

> "5. This is what the Sovereign Lord says: This is Jerusalem, which I have set in the center of the nations., with countries all around her. 6. Yet in her wickedness she has rebelled against my laws and decrees more than the nations and the

countries around her. She has rejected my laws and has not followed my decrees. 7. Therefore, this is what the Sovereign Lord says: You have been more unruly than the nations around you and have not followed my decrees or kept my laws. You have not even conformed to the standards of the nations around you. 8. Therefore this is what the Sovereign Lord says: I myself am against you, Jerusalem, and I will inflict punishment on you and will scatter you in the sight of the nations. 9. Because of all your detestable idols, **I will do to you what I have never done before and will never do again.** 10. Therefore in your midst fathers will eat their children, and children will eat their fathers. I will inflict punishment on you and will scatter all your survivors to the winds. 11. Therefore as surely as I live, declares the Sovereign Lord, because you have defiled my sanctuary with all your vile images and detestable practices, I myself will withdraw my favor; I will not look on you with pity or spare you" (NIV).

It was not as if Jesus was glad about casting the nation into the sea and leaving them desolate. Remember our Lord's lament in Matthew 23: 37 (NIV) – "Jerusalem, Jerusalem, you who kill the prophets and stone those sent to you, how often I have longed to gather your children together, as a hen gathers her chicks under her wings, but you were not willing." However, like with the flood, God will not have to destroy His chosen nation again in like manner. His Kingdom is now within.

To read some fascinating accounts, and I do mean fascinating historical accounts from Josephus and others, I encourage you to read Dr. Gentry's book, "The Olivet Discourse Made Easy" or Grady Brown's book, "That All May Be Fulfilled". Some of the historical details offered by eyewitnesses will make the hair stand up on the back of your neck, and they will also bring tears to your eyes due to the suffering, including cannibalism, incurred by those who did not heed our Lord's warnings.

Josephus estimated that 1.1 million people died during the overtaking of the city and the destruction of the temple by the Romans. This was the capital of the country that God had chosen to usher in His kingdom. These were the people who were offered the kingdom when Jesus came as their Messiah – "The kingdom of heaven is at hand." And these are the people over whom He wept after they rejected Him. These are the people who crucified Him.

I believe this is why Matthew applies our Lord's stern words to their "generation" at least nine times. However, some take the last reference to their generation in chapter 24 and push it out literally thousands of years to make it fit their understanding. They do the same with Daniel's 70 weeks, which were "determined" to last 70 weeks. Personally, I never understood the creation of a gap in Daniel's prophecy; it never made any sense to me.

However, I did struggle for years wondering if Jesus, in the Olivet Discourse, was speaking about events far into the future. At last, after taking my questions to our Father, I feel comfortable that there are no gaps in the words of Jesus either. When He referred to their generation, He meant it.

Many futurist views also presuppose that God's plan includes the fulfillment of certain promises made to the ethnic Jewish nation of Israel, as they are used to establish God's kingdom on the earth sometime in the future. However, consider what Jesus said of that fig tree: "May you never bear fruit again" (Matthew 21:19, NIV), and of Jerusalem: "Look, your house is left unto you desolate" (Matthew 23:38, NIV).

Secondly, the words of Paul are quite clear: "And if you belong to Christ, then you are Abraham's seed and heirs according to the promise" (Galatians 3:29, NIV). He repeats this same theme in several other passages as well. Citizenship in God's Kingdom is no longer about ethnicity. I believe that Jesus still loves Israel greatly, and His unrelenting love will not fail them. However, it appears these former enemies will be in the third group in God's order of men to be made alive. The ones chosen first shall be the last ones to enter, but they do enter.

Again, I am not a preterist, but I appreciate the research presented by Ken, Grady, and others for our benefit and consideration. I met Ken in South Carolina, and I found him to be very helpful with my questions. I thank our Father for the work He has done through him and the help he has given me.

My final advice: When scriptures do not appear to line up perfectly, admit it, and be honest with Him. Then, humbly ask for His help. Afterwards, relax and wait for Him to clarify things. We know that He is the best teacher ever! Sometimes, His answers come overnight, and other times, it may take years. During the waiting period, rest comfortably knowing that He will provide a better understanding at exactly the right time for you.

ABOUT THE AUTHOR

JIM STRAHAN graduated from St. Mary's University in San Antonio, Texas, where he received a degree in mathematics and physics. Afterward, he had a rewarding and successful career as an Industrial Engineer at UPS. After UPS, he retired a second time from The University of Texas at San Antonio, where he managed their transportation department. He is married and has been blessed with two children and five grandchildren.

While being transferred across the country with UPS, he served as a deacon, elder, and teacher in churches he attended. While working for UTSA, he was able to co-host a Christian radio show for a year and wrote a book called "The Brightness Around Him." He also co-authored another book, "Is God Fair? What about Gandhi?"

In retirement, He loves to play golf and teach his grandchildren to fish. Even more, he loves to read books by other Christians, and study God's Word.

At the age of seven, Jesus revealed Himself to Jim in a very special way. As a result, Jim believes this book is the one he was born to write. He also believes that God is writing all of our stories, and one day, looking back with clarity, we will be able to see His miraculous intervention in all of our lives, as He was molding and shaping us into His image and likeness.

Printed in the United States
by Baker & Taylor Publisher Services